Checklist of Civilizations and Culture

Checklist of Civilizations and Culture

A. L. Kroeber

With a new introduction by Lionel Tiger

Routledge
Taylor & Francis Group
LONDON AND NEW YORK

Originally published in 1962 by the Wenner-Gren Foundation for Anthropological Research

Published 2011 by Transaction Publishers

Published 2017 by Routledge
2 Park Square, Milton Park, Abingdon, Oxon OX14 4RN
711 Third Avenue, New York, NY 10017, USA

Routledge is an imprint of the Taylor & Francis Group, an informa business

Library of Congress Catalog Number: 2011004426

Library of Congress Cataloging-in-Publication Data

Kroeber, A. L. (Alfred Louis), 1876-1960.
Checklist of civilizations and culture / A. L. Kroeber.
p. cm.
Originally published: New York : Wenner-Gren Foundation for Anthropological Research, 1962.
ISBN 978-1-4128-1853-7
1. Civilization, Western. 2. Civilization--History. I. Title.

CB59.K7 2011
909'.09821--dc22

2011004426

ISBN 13: 978-1-4128-1853-7 (pbk)

CONTENTS

INTRODUCTION TO THE TRANSACTION EDITION

A.F. Kroeber was a master anthropological theorist and commentator. This book is a collection of his writing on broad cultural themes and historical processes. It serves as a tour de force of ur-history, and while Prof. Kroeber's choices of emphasis may be personal and eccentric, nevertheless we benefit from a synthetic and learned guide. Rather unusually for workaday anthropologists, we find ourselves contemplating *BigThink* scholars such as Toynbee, Spengler, and Danilevsky. Kroeber navigates among such proponents of huge analysis by suggesting an integrative template which reflects his decades of anthropological experience.

Reading the book is like attending a performance of a Bach cello concerto. The experience is of artfulness, dedication, and reinterpretation of what is known, not a bold experiment. It is a concert rather than a scientific assertion. It is not about what is new, about the latest mathematical explanation of everything or the Parisian Left Bank gilding of a suffocated anthropological lily. And like any treasure of human thought or art or scholarship, it is worth protecting its existence, in this case, in the form of the book you hold in your hands. So thank the publisher, even if your taste doesn't run to efforts to decide whether certain communities boasted high culture while others were just struggling on the way up.

For example, Kroeber provides a sequence of interesting and stimulating commentary about the transition from shamanism to priesthood. Nearly everyone will find something or much with which to dispute Kroeber's narrative here. While some scholars will decide that the discussion is hopeless and worthless, nevertheless for many students of religion and just citizens the subject remains intellectually vibrant, to say nothing of politically and socially significant. Nothing adventured, nothing gained or lost. And who are priests anyway and why do communities pay their rent?

Sometimes big questions involve small personal or communal matters. Hard sledding though it may seem to some, Kroeber reminds us that the day-to-day is embedded in the year-to-year and millennium to millennium. He reminds us also that anthropology was for a long time one of the broadest and most ambitious of disciplines. And when *BigThink* meets direct and muscular analysis of specific places and events, such as in his analysis of Pueblo culture in United States, it becomes clear that the assumptions of even modest thought disguise often jumbo presuppositions. In fact, his treatment of these North American people, with their South American connections, offers some of the most rewarding reading in this otherwise dry catalogue and evaluation.

At the methodological level, an interesting feature of Kroeber's perspective redounds from his perception that Darwin's assertion about interconnectedness between early and late organisms had a rather decisively stimulating impact on social scientists. They craved a master diachronic theory, just like the biologists. That search carries on, despite the explanatory barriers thrown up by forms of post-modern discourse and the partisans of nature-culture as the true metric of human sociality.

Kroeber also revisits some core assumptions about the anthropology of language, with an intriguing sortie into analysis of that special linguistic form, poetry. What does it mean and how does oratorical Arabic differ from Walt Whitman's characteristic verse and with what consequence? As well, even the advanced civilization of the old near East lacked what he considered poetry, which precedes yet another reflection which is elegant and also unarguable. Agree or not, the effort is absorbing.

This describes a satisfying portion of this very special collection of papers and perceptions.

Lionel Tiger
Charles Darwin Professor of Anthropology, Emeritus,
Rutgers University

PREFACE

In 1957, Professor Kroeber began to set down in outline and introductory, though concrete, form the material that comprises his "Roster of Civilizations and Culture." Though encouraged and strongly urged on by friends and colleagues, other commitments and activities intervened, and he was unable to complete the task he had set for himself. The material here presented is that which Kroeber left in his file marked Roster of Civilizations. Editorial activity has seemed mostly gratuitous and has been kept at a minimum. The material has been arranged in the fashion which Kroeber's outline and common sense dictated. Some of the sections, such as the Introduction and that on Minor Civilizations in North America, were in completed form and needed nothing save perhaps an omitted place or name, which have been added as brackets indicate. Other sections, such as those on Science and Divination, were scarcely begun. It seemed well to include them because they are pertinent to the more complete material included here and because they further clarify what Kroeber had in mind. These sketches are reproduced in italics, exactly as he left them. The square brackets appearing in the Table of Contents are reproduced from the original manuscript and presumably indicate some uncertainty in Professor Kroeber's mind as to what the final heading should be.

Two sections, *Presences and Absences: Old and New World Civilizations* and *Time Profile,* are included here as appendices. Though they obviously are not a part of the Substantive Roster, Kroeber included them in the file with the other material. They are complete in themselves; that they are pertinent to "A Roster of Civilizations and Culture" is obvious.

Charles A. Le Guin

In making the difficult decisions as to what most properly to do with the considerable materials contained under "work in progress" in Kroeber's files, that which is fragmentary and lacking the author's own "finishing" for the most part, will not be published, but will become part of the Kroeber manuscript archives. The decision to publish A ROSTER OF CIVILIZATIONS AND CULTURE rests upon the "finishedness" of its few completed parts, and its accessibility to continuation and elaboration on the part of other culture historians who may be stimulated from time to time to add to these small but varied beginnings.

THEODORA K. KROEBER

INTRODUCTION

HEREWITH is submitted a sort of checklist of the known principal civilizations and cultures of the world, with such definition as is possible of their area and time, their subdivisions and periods, and a skeleton indication of their character.

The terms civilization and culture are used here not contrastively or exclusively, but inclusively as essential synonyms of sometimes varying accent. There is no difference of principle between the two words: they denote somewhat distinguishable grades of degree of the same thing. Civilization currently carries an overtone of high development of a society; culture has become the customary term of universal denotation in this range, applicable alike to high or low products and heritages of societies. Every human society has its culture, complex or simple. The word culture could therefore be properly used to include all the particular exemplars that will be listed; but for the larger and richer cultures the term civilization has current usage, and need not be quarrelled with, on the understanding that no distinctions of kind between civilization and culture are implied.

The unqualified term culture is *not* used here to denote any part of the total culture of a human society, such as the higher or spiritual or more cultivable segment.

This component or segment of culture or civilization can be denoted as "value culture," on the ground of having value, or being an end in itself, and not merely means to practical ends. It includes all purely aesthetic and intellectual activity; but without being rigorously delimited to such activity. It certainly includes an element in every religion, though religions usually also contain organization and institutionalization; and it includes some part of morals, though morality is directed also to personal conduct and action.

What is called "creativity" coincides pretty closely with a concern for value culture as just defined: aesthetic and intellectual operations, the allied parts of religion and ethics, and perhaps other segments, or facies of segments, of total culture. In general usage the terms cultural and culture connote this concept. A compound term, "fine-culture," might be coined to denote it, on the precedent of fine arts, belles lettres, and pure science.

Creative or value culture must be conceived and dealt with as (1) represented by objective phenomena and as (2) an operationally useful concept. It is not set off from the rest of culture by any non-experiential or ineffable property or quality or by spirit, soul, or deity.

The many past and present cultures grade into one another in space and time in a vast continuum. There are no absolute breaks, and a minority of marked or decisive ones, in human culture. This is as clear as are the unity and the continuity which historians assume as axiomatic of human history. In fact the two principles are in one sense facets of each other, since culture is always accompanied by, and due to, historic events, and on the other hand events can occur only in a given matrix of culture and in turn rest upon this.

This makes the partitive segregation or delimitation of cultures and civilizations a far from simple matter. It requires wide knowledge, a willingness to compare and balance, the ability to discern distinctions of pattern and to rise above elemental disparate facts. Delimitation of culture corresponds closely to periodization in history, which is also an end-product of learning and of judgment by consensus. Both processes, the delimitation of cultures (or the recognition of their identity) and periodization in history, are organizations of the almost endless continuum of culture and of historical happening; and they aid in orderly and significant apprehension of the phenomena dealt with.

The need for such apprehension often weighs lightly on the specialist or devotee of one period or country or province; but the need becomes more urgent as interest becomes more broadly comparative or philosophical. Both narrow and broad interests are of course legitimate: there should be no conflict between them: each can aid and advance the other.

No scheme of classification of periods or cultures can hope to be final or irrevocably demonstrable: their classification will always be in the state of being remodeled. Historians realize that history is ever being "rewritten"—that is, reinterpreted—which fact sooner or later entails its reperiodization or reclassification also. The same holds for the understanding of total human culture by anthropologists, archaeologists, and culture historians: its growths, interrelations, and organized classification will always be reformulated, on the basis of new knowledge, new ideas, and new points of view.

It is this everlasting reformulation that has worried so acute a theorist as the late R. G. Collingwood into occupying the illogically defeatist position of seeing all periods or "cycles"—he means not repetitions but differentiable larger developments—as "illusory." They spring from special interest in some culmination or cluster of events, he says, which is then extended forward and backward until less knowledge and interest cause a bound to be set to the "cycle"; which boundary however is not in the phenomena but is essentially one of relative ignorance. This, Collingwood says, is proved by subsequent students each seeing the limits of the cycle (read: period or culture) differently. Since no objective determination of cycle limits is possible, cycles are therefore [*sic*] illusory. In other words, to Collingwood human history is forever condemned to remain an undifferentiable magma, a movement in time of unorganizable events—the flow of an endless river of gravel, might be a fair simile. This ultra-negativism probably springs from a hyper-perfectionism, from the desire to reach an objectivity such as even physics cannot achieve; and, on realization that such an attainment is impossible, there is rejection of all conceptual organization of the material of human history.

Contrariwise, most historians and anthropologists are relativists. They accept, tacitly or overtly, that no conceptualization of history or culture is absolute or final, that it normally has some greater or less value, and that while no interpretation can hope to endure forever unmodified, findings of new significance, however overlain by later formulations or incorporated into them, can be influential for a very long time, either directly or as a precondition of fuller and deeper understanding. Newly formulated significances can give the stream of historical thinking a new direction, or at least produce in it a bend or riffle or pool.

The problem of the sound recognition—the intellectually profitable recognition—of periods and cultures, is a relativistic one. In simplest terms, it deals with recognizing where the greater similarities and the greater differences occur in the data dealt with, and what these similarities and differences are. Essentially the problem is one of classification, of conceptual organization of the raw facts. The facts ordinarily come to us in history organized only in terms of place and time and individual personality, whereas in much of culture history and archaeology, determination of time is part of the problem and the persons involved may never be ascertainable. Yet the task of finding meaning in the facts of history and of culture is similar in principle.

At bottom, the classification of history and culture seems bound also to be somewhat like the classification of the forms of life. Species of animals and plants change so much more slowly than human cultures as to appear at first sight as fixed and constant. With the time factor seemingly absent, classification of organisms looks relatively simple, and some rude germs of classification can be discerned in the lexicon even of primitive peoples. Certainly Aristotle already made what is in effect a classification of phyla—not a very successful effort, but also not too bad for a beginning. Linnaeus began his *Systema Naturae* in 1735 and followed in 1753 with *Species Plantarum*. These works were a roster of the then known or recognized organisms inhabiting our planet, each assigned a description in an international language and a two-part name intended to make permanent and indubitable identification possible; and the elemental species were grouped successively into genera, families, orders, and on up, so that every organism had its coordinated and superordinated place in a system which at least aimed at being total for living forms on earth. Linnaeus's knowledge—or rather, that of his day—was necessarily very incomplete; necessarily also it was deficient as regards much internal structure; and in arriving at its organization, his classification varied between shrewd commonsense and artificial or arbitrary considerations. But it was at least like a motion before the house of science, which could be amended, enlarged, improved. Almost immediately this deepening and correcting began, leading to a "natural classification," that is, one based on all the intrinsic properties and structures of organisms so far as they could be recognized, in place of extrinsic considerations of logic, reason, caprice, or vulgar custom. By the time of Cuvier, halfway to Darwin, this natural classification was well under way; and Cuvier's fundamental types of organization—based on comparative anatomy, that is, structure—were approaching the phyla, the largest organic groupings recognized today.

So far, the tacit assumption was of an organic world essentially static since its creation. With Darwinism, the conceptual dam had finally collapsed, the dimension of time was accepted as axiomatic as it had long been for human history, and the history or "evolution" of life was therewith recognized as a task corresponding to the history of man. In fact, acceptance of organic evolution came with a great bound, because, both living and fossil forms of life being abundantly available for structural analysis, their classification had been made so well in the days of pre-dynamic biological research that this classification could be taken over almost bodily into evolutionary doctrine, with mutual profit. Each basic type of structure or "phylum" proved to be one of the basic lines of evolution, so that its significance was much deepened; and reciprocally, the classification was so much ready-made, marshalled evidence in support and proof of the evolutionary doctrine.

Human history is of course in an inverse position. Instead of becoming dynamic only as of 1859, it has always had and dealt with time as a factor; but it has had no classification. Indeed, classifications of phenomena as they occur dynamically in nature are inherently difficult to attain to—far harder than static classifications. To be sure there is another kind of dynamic analysis, that which looks for *process*, which is readily feasible once a beginning has been made. But it is feasible through leading the phenomena into a laboratory of experimentation, where they are insulated, controlled, and varied one at a time; and no such laboratory is available for the data of history which lie in the past, nor scarcely for the data of culture which, especially as they approach the holistic, are untransplantable.

It is no wonder that historians in general have renounced classification except of the most obvious and common-knowledge sort, as by countries or continents or by large periods as these became convenient for orientation, and that they have emphasized the continuity of their phenomena. They must be granted full competence in the analytic penetration of their material; but by and large they do not attempt its formal organization: certainly not by way of systematic classification. Instead, they usually convey their analysis while presenting a selection of their data in narration, or, not infrequently, in topical description of a moment or cross-section of the temporal flow.

There is no question that classification of the data of history is inherently difficult. Whether it is impossible, or if possible is limited in scope and in what way, is something I shall return to discuss.

Meanwhile, other and later students of man, substituting for events the consideration of institutions, or of the forms of societies, and of the cultural products of these societies, were really facing patterns which in principle at least might be treated statically and might be classifiable. Among such students the anthropologists have most consistently examined sociocultural units as they seem to occur more or less segregated in nature and history.

The first generation of anthropologists, unleashed in 1859 by *The Origin of Species,* were fired by a great enthusiasm and the vision of discovering a principle or set of principles about human beings comparable to the ideas of Natural Selection and Evolution about animals and plants. They set off cross country, leaping all gates in full hue and cry, and had an exciting ride. There were few results to show at the end of it, for they had not, like the biologists, inherited a ready-made but intensive and careful classification of their subject matter; nor did they, in the quest for grand principles, attach any serious significance even to the particular and commonly known groupings of societies and cultures as these had grown up in the world, and which, in their total given similarities and dissimilarities, would seem to provide a mass of data that might be more or less successfully classifiable.

Later anthropologists did turn to such naturally provided societies and cultures as their subject of investigation. This was a much more modest and sober undertaking. More and more it came to be felt that these natural aggregations were phenomena worthy of study in themselves, not merely as opportunities from which exemplifications of some ingenious idea or transcendent principle might be luckily looted.

With this there grew a respect for the phenomena in the matrix of their occurrence, for the given sociocultural aggregates, each in its totality. There was even for a while a "functional" school of anthropology which stressed the totalities by dissecting out the network of the inner connections of each. The larger cultures, most often called civilizations, were too massive for a single scholar to treat in this way: generations of Hellenists, Egyptologists, Sinologists had been at their cultures and were still working. But societies of the size of tribes, and possessing cultures of limited scope, did seem to warrant hope that they could be known with reasonable accuracy and characterized holistically.

This was of course not the only stream of interest and activity in anthropology concerned with living peoples. There is also the interest in process as such, as discernible in culture change; or in grasping its psychological or individualistic aspects; and such studies could often be better pursued in a smaller context or field than a whole culture. But systematic ethnography did tend to view cultures as wholes, and from that to pass on to viewing them in their interrelations, both as to the spread and interflow of their content, and as to their adjacencies and similarities and groupings.

A step in this direction was the recognition of "culture areas," regions of comparatively similar or common culture. These were most readily established where the absence of historic records, and of archaeological findings or search, presented a seemingly static picture. Such culture area classifications were somewhat comparable to the pre-Darwinian taxonomies of the animal and plant kingdoms; and like them, they contained an implicit developmental history. In both cases, actual developmental data—from palaeontology, archaeology, historic documents—might upset the classifications, and did regularly correct them, but also tended to enrich and firm them. One reason descriptive ethnographies have often been found dull reading even by anthropologists is that, like taxonomic biological descriptions, they rarely are intended as an end in themselves, but are always a means toward a larger end —of the recognition of interrelations of forms, or "systematic" classification.

It must be admitted that systematic developmental classification of the lower or backward cultures (corresponding roughly say to the invertebrates in the animal kingdom) has not been carried as far or pursued as energetically by ethnographers as might be. There have been many other lines of interest, the profession is after all a small one, and so on. The body of the present essay does include an effort at such a classification of the non-literate cultures—skeletonized of necessity, but as systematic and as complete in coverage as possible.

I regard such a formulation as one of the things that the world of learning has a right to expect from anthropology. It is one of our responsibilities.

As for the literate or large cultures usually called civilizations, their internal classification must of course be made basically by their historians: both "historians" as such, and those regionally qualified, like Semiticists, Sinologists, etc. Obviously only those specialists with fairly developed comparative interest or bent are likely to contribute much to a "classification"—which of course, so far as information permits, is also a family tree, precisely as in modern biology.

The historian who has contributed most in this direction is of course Toynbee; but he has had predecessors and competitors, mostly non-historians.

I exclude from present consideration all philosophies of history, as being selective instead of cumulative in the materials treated. The problem of recognizing the world's cultures is essentially one of natural history, and involves dealing with all the phenomena and then building up their patterns or classes step by step. When this historical construct has been achieved, even in rough or preliminary form, there will be much room and need for philosophizing about it; but the time is after, not before.

There has long been a semi-learned interest in the succession of empires, a dramatizing or moralizing concern with their rise and fall. This has influenced on the one hand the choice of literary-scholarly subjects like Gibbon's *Decline and Fall;* on the other, it has led to prophets of doom such as Spengler. Even Toynbee, who is a superscholar, has been affected. He does not predict the collapse of civilization as inevitable, but he is concerned and moralizes about it. That we shall shortly return to barbarism and anarchy is exciting news if true; but too much such preoccupation with the future, or how it can be saved, is calculated to disturb our understanding of the past and present.

Another and related preoccupation that must be avoided is the assumption that civilizations occur with a definite life course similar to that of individual organisms. This idea had its roots in eighteenth-century universal histories, became connected with the succession or rise-and-fall-of-empires assumption, was systematically developed by Danilevsky and dogmatically exaggerated by Spengler. Culminations of cultural activity, with their rises and declines, do tend to suggest that cultures as well as organisms may have a normal life course or trajectory. Certainly many styles of creativity appear to run such a course, and the idea may be extensible to whole cultures. But this is something to be investigated, not assumed as a premise and then proved by the selected cases that fit the assumption.

SUBSTANTIVE ROSTER

SUBSTANTIVE ROSTER

[Professor Kroeber's Roster is divided into five categories, as the following outline indicates. Categories 11–39 were to be devoted to Asia, though Kroeber's outline begins with 21 and ends with 30. No indication remains of what he intended for categories 11 through 20 or 31 through 39.]

1–10: EUROPE

*1. *Classic, Graeco-Roman, Hellenic*
2. *Western, Occidental, European*
*[3.] *Megalithic*
*4. *Keltic*
*5. *Norse*
[6.] *Russian*

* *Extinct*

11–39: ASIA

[21–23]
24. *Ancient Near Eastern Civil.*
25. *Islam*
26. *India Tibet—B[urma] and Siam—Ceylon—Indonesia*
27. *Sinic Korea—Japan—Annam*
28. *C[entral] Asian Steppes—Induced Civiliz.*
29. *Peripheral N. Cult.—Taiga, Tundra, and Maritime*
[30.] *Southern Prim. Cult.—remnant enclaves in forest and mts.*

40–49: OCEANIA

44. Austr[alia]
41. N[ew] G[uinea]
42. Melanesia
43. Micronesia
44. Polynesia

50–59: AFRICA

50. Egypt
[51.] Nubian-Ethiopic-Hamitic sphere of cult. and semi-civiliz. with e.g. Christian, Islamic religions and funct.
[52.] Saharan cultures
53. W. African Negro cultures
54. E. and S. African cattle cultures
55. S. African remnant cultures
[56.] Medit. littoral (orig. Sah. ??)
>Gr. Phoen.
>Roman
>Islamic

60–69: NEW WORLD

60. Mexican Civilization—Calendrical and glyph. core
61. S. W.
Anasazi-Hohokam >Pueblo core
Pima-Tumai-Sonora
62. Eastern and Northern
a. Hopewell—B. m. Mississippi—y Cofed.—d. Plains
A. Agricultural core
B. Non Agr. Mex-Tex-Plains core
C. " " N. Hunting
63. Desert—Steppe—Plateau—Intermontane Core—Calif. 2 foci
65. [sic] N. W. Coast
66. Eskimo

EUROPE 1–10

I. CLASSIC, HELLENIC, GRAECO-ROMAN, OR MEDITERRANEAN CIVILIZATION

PHASES

ALPHA. *Minoan, Minoan-Mycenaean, Aegean.* —1800 or earlier to —1200. Crete, S. Greek islands, Argolis, Attica, Boeotia. Recent evidence makes it appear that the area was already Greek-speaking, at least in part, in Minoan times. One Cretan (?) fragment of population became the Philistines. The culture is too well known to need characterization here; its similarity to Classic Greek civilization is evident in seaward orientation, architecture, art, religion.

ALPHA-BETA INTERVAL. —1200 to —900. Aesthetic retrogression on mainland and islands, confusion, movements of population, Doric invasions.

BETA. *Greek.* —900 to —197/190/146/31.

Beta 1. Hellenic city states dominant to —338, extinguished in —146, (Tarentum —272, Syracuse —212).

Beta 2. Hellenistic kingdoms dominant in Macedon and western Asia —338 to —190, extinguished —31. Hellenistic "common" culture and speech dominant in government and on the upper levels of society in Asia Minor, Syria, Egypt until incorporation in Roman empire, a process essentially completed in —31. The culture (Christianized), and Greek speech in upper strata, continued in Syria and Egypt until Islamic conquest 638, 641, and N of Taurus until loss to Turks at Manzikert in 1071.

PRE-GAMMA. *Etruscan, Tyrrhenian.* 800 to 300/200. Influenced by Greeks; in art, especially 550–475, and 300 seq.; influencing Rome generally until 400 or after.

GAMMA. *Roman.* "—753"/500 ± to 330/476. City-state republic until —31, then (principate and) empire. Italic Latin origins, absorptions from Greeks of S Italy and Etruscans till 300; general Hellenic-Hellenistic influence more systematic in —III to —I C. Gradual conquest of Italy, Mediterranean Africa, Iberia, Gaul, most of Britain, parts of S Germany, Austria, Hungary, with imposition of Latin culture and speech, and permanent retention of Latin speech in Iberia and Gaul. Disintegration of empire began in III C, especially in W or Latin half. In (IV) V C, invasions of Alaric, Genseric, Attila, Visigoths, Clovis tore off territory. Only the bishopric of Rome (>Papacy) retained primacy.

DELTA. *Byzantine.* 330–1453. From the removal of the empire's capital to New Rome (Constantinople) to its fall to the Osmanli Turks. The E half of the empire, thoroughly Christianized, was retained essentially intact until Islam, Illyria being the only Latin-speaking area. Latin remained the language of government and law through VI C. Christianized Hellenic culture was retained with remarkable conservatism and civilized effectiveness, but cultural creativity remained astonishingly low, the aesthetic and intellectual renaissances under the militarily expansive emperors (Justinian, Heraclius, 527–65, 610–41 and the Macedonians, 867–1057) being barely perceptible. Turks took most of Anatolia in 1071, and after the capture of Constantinople by the Frankish or "Latin" Fourth Crusade in 1204, the "Roman" empire of Byzantium was reduced to a splinter. A convincing periodization is by Ostrogorsky, summarized below.

[EPSILON, *Modern Greece*, 1827 on, is hardly a legitimate fifth phase, after submergence for four centuries; also because Greek culture has become basically Western, though with some Levantine persistences, and a fierce retention of Greek speech.]

Philip Bagby, in *Culture and History*, 1958, pages 167–168, includes Byzantium as well as modern Greece in a "Near Eastern" civilization, which consists mostly of Islamic peoples, but includes minor Christian and other sects. I presume that Mohammedans speaking Arabic, Persian, and Osmanli Turkish would belong, and that those speaking Hamitic, Urdu, Malaysian languages would be excluded by their geography.

This is avowedly Spengler's Magian or Arabic culture, somewhat enlarged, and emerging according to Bagby about +I C, but becoming dominant in eastern Roman empire only in IV C. The classification of civilizations in the Near East (southwest Asia) is difficult, and its consideration must be reserved for its proper place below; but as to any Near Eastern culture including Byzantium, I do not agree with Bagby. There are resemblances, of course, as he points out: there always are where there is long-term propinquity; but they seem not to hold at the most critical points. The orientation of Byzantine civilization was Christian, Hellenic, and Roman; it was anti-Iranian, anti-Mohammedan, anti-inner Asian, as it was anti-western and anti-barbarian. Its productive creativity had shriveled, but it clung tenaciously to its inherited civilized past, because it was by what it retained of that past that it maintained itself. It may have been an unduly belated past, but this past was the core of the civilization.

Areas and Subareas

A. Hellenic City-states.

1. Greece and near-by islands.
2. West coast of Anatolia and adjacent islands, with much influence from and then on Lydia, Caria, Lycia before and after 500.
3. Crete: relatively unimportant in post-Minoan phases. In part of Cyprus, there was a substandard version of Hellenic culture.
4. Magna Graecia: S Italian coast, E half of Sicily.

5–7. Remote outposts, significant for the spread of Greek influence: 5) Naucratis, to Egypt, Cyrene, to the Lybians; 6) Black Sea colonies, to Scythians; 7) Marseilles, to the Gauls.

B. Hellenistic Asia and Egypt: as the result of Alexander's conquests, and retention of much of these by his successors. In spite of Greek dynasties maintaining themselves for a while in spots in Bactria and W India, the main area E of the Euphrates was lost to Hellenism within a century of Alexander, but Asia Minor, Syria, and Egypt remained Hellenistic on the upper levels of their culture under Hellenistic kings and after them as part of Rome.

C. Italic Latin Rome. As this city-state conquest-republic took over

Latium, Campania, Italy, and finally all the Mediterranean lands, it accepted Greek creative culture almost *in toto*, and added its own originations in government, law, and engineering, thus broadening and solidifying the original Hellenic achievement. When the last Roman contribution had been made, and Christianity was within a century of its prevalence, the culture, economics, and empire began to disintegrate sharply in the Latin West, but were preserved in the Greek East.

Appendix

*Ostrogorsky's Periodization of Byzantine History**

I. Early Byzantine, 324–610.
 a. To 378, defeat of Adrianople. More important than the rule changes of 395 or 476.
 b. To 518.
 c. To 610. Justinian's reconquest of Africa, Italy, and S Spain from Germans; then disorder. Antiquity ends.

II. Middle Byzantine, 610–1025. Heraclius: reconquests and reforms. Themes instituted. Army of settled stratiotes. Greek becomes official language. Emperor: "basileus." Didaskaleion: university, clerical origin.
 a. To 718, repulse of second Arab siege of Constantinople.
 b. To 843, settlement of Iconoclastic controversy.
 c. To 1025, end of Macedonian dynasty, 867–1025. Slavic missions; Photios against Rome. Sea power wrested back from Arabs (2nd 1/2 X C). State control of industry and commerce.

III. Late Byzantine, 1025–1453.
 a. To 1081. Control by civilian aristocracy. 1071, Manzikert, Anatolia lost to Turks, S Italy to Normans. Depreciation of currency, 1078–1118.
 b. To 1204. 1082, loss of sea power, cession to Venice. Military revival, Alexios I; feudalism; tax collection leased.
 [Latin Empire of Constantinople, 1204–61.]
 c. 1261–82. Michael VIII. Revival.

* Based on G. Ostrogorsky, "Die Perioden der Byzantinischen Geschichte," *Historische Zeitschrift*, 163:237–254, 1901.

d. To 1453. Decline to minor power under Andronikos II, 1282–1328. Advance of Ottomans and Serbs. Venice and Genoa crowd Byzantium off sea. It becomes a vassal realm of the Turks.

2. WESTERN, OCCIDENTAL, OR EUROPEAN CIVILIZATION

("European" in contrast with Classic-Mediterranean)

Phases

Pre-Alpha. *Dark Ages*, or latter part of them, including Carolingian period. "476"/500 or c. 650 to 900/950. Toynbee (1:40) once set 775 as the beginning: before then he reckons western Europe as still in "Hellenic" (Roman) civilization. Spengler's tabulation gives 500–900 for the prodromal period or "Spring" of the new civilization. If the Dark Age nadir of disintegration could be determined, it would obviously serve as the adequate point of inception of the new civilization. My ±650 is a tentative stab at this nadir. The Hegira, 622, which is certainly significant in Asia, would obviously also not be far off from the lowest ebb in the West.

Two events of influence on the future happened in the latter part of this pre-Alpha period: establishment of the Carolingian empire over most of western Christian Europe. This was the first large-scale, temporarily successful political fabric since the disintegration of the Roman West (and the last political union of essentially the whole of West European civilization). The second event was the emergence of writing of the vernacular languages (Strasbourg oaths, etc.). The recognition of these vernaculars was of course a precondition of their subsequent literatures and of the still later slow development of nationalism.

Alpha. *Latin Mediaeval Europe*, Western Middle Ages. 900/950 to 1300/1325. "High Middle Ages" is the term usually applied to the XII–XIII C culmination. The First Crusade, 1096–99, evidenced an already developed expansive potential in the Mediaeval West. In *Configurations*, 757, I estimated the cultural climax of the Mediaeval phase to fall close to 1250. By 1300–1325 the peak had been passed in architecture, sculpture, scholastic philosophy, and literature, and the Church was encountering attacks and dissensions, beginning with the coup at

Anagni in 1304. The center of the Alpha phase was France; Italy's participation was sidelong or secondary.

ALPHA-BETA INTERVAL. *Late Middle Ages.* 1300/25 to c. 1515 in France and N (to 1400/25 in Italy). This was the first reconstitution of Western civilization, with decay of the Catholic-provincial-feudal patterns of the High Mediaeval phase, but growth of population (in spite of setback by Black Death), wealth, technology (printing, etc.), knowledge, and extension of geographical horizons.

BETA. *Renaissance-Modern.* C. 1515 to c. 1910 (but in Italy from 1400–25 on). In creative activities, the lead lay with Italy for nearly two centuries, then shifted to trans-Alpine Europe: successively France, Holland, Britain, Germany. Political hegemony was attempted (always unsuccessfully) by Spain, then by France, with Germany on the verge of making the try at the end of the phase. Russia (with Byzantine influence on it ended) slowly "entered Europe" in this phase, with heavy acceleration under Peter the Great and political participation in XVIII C and creative participation in XIX. Extra-European colonial extensions of the civilization, most importantly and permanently in the Americas, coincided with the phase, but these new areas had acquired little political and less recognized aesthetic-intellectual influence in the European center by the end of the period. The end date ("c. 1910") is still too near ourselves to be fixed with assurance. The beginning at "1515" is a try at a date which more or less covers the attainment of culmination of visual art in Italy, the beginning of the spread of this art over Europe, and the Reformation in the North.

SUBPERIODS OF BETA. It is evident that the four modern centuries group into two main periods, but the demarcation can be set somewhat variably. The first period contains the permanent split of Western Christianity through the Reformation, plus "religious" wars ending in 1648 (1660/88 in England); and this is probably the commonest conventional historiographic subperiodization. The second subphase is certainly by contrast one of rationalism, enlightenment, and secularization, with growing middle-class influence. Relative landmarks in creative activities are: around or by 1700, all the greatest manifestations of

Renaissance-Baroque painting and sculpture are over; modern music begins; first phase of originating modern Western science ends, followed by a relative lull. Around 1750, a second phase of science opens, with marked increase of experiment, systematized observation in the earth and life sciences, tending toward a historic approach, and the rapid development of adequate qualitative attack in chemistry; definitive abandonment of Latin in favor of vernaculars as the vehicle of science; beginning of modern German literature; and beginning of the industrial revolution in England.

BETA-GAMMA INTERVAL. *Second Reconstitution* (?): 1910 onward. Existing aesthetic style patterns definitely attacked and disrupted; World Wars I, II, tensions in most aspects of the civilization; but population, wealth, communication, industry, science still expanding vigorously, and the culture spreading rapidly to the "empty" areas of America, Australasia, Africa, and tending to supplant native cultures and transform old native civilizations in Asia and Africa. Two efforts at hegemony by Germany failed at the beginning of the interval. Russia, after a revolution, is now making the same bid; but this attempt is *de facto* only a competing variant within the civilization, and of it. It is definitely not the building of a new and replacing civilization, since the successful culture of contemporary Russia emanates from Western civilization and on the whole is by 1960 increasingly assimilating to it. The counterpoise to Russia in resources and strength is the United States, British-derived in history, speech, and culture. The center of power and wealth productivity thus has definitely moved out of western-central Europe to the peripheral East and West; and there are indications that the East and West may come to dominate in creativity also; although so far there has possibly been less growth of creativity at the two flanks than dying away of its forms in the old West-European center.

It is of course still uncertain whether this Beta-Gamma interval will prove to be a reconstruction to a new phase (Gamma) within Western civilization, or a larger interval between it and a future basically new and distinct civilization. The latter alternative seems somewhat the less likely because of the growth which continues successfully in so many segments of the existing Western culture—in contrast to the inter-Classic-Western interval of the Dark Ages, which was almost wholly retractile or disintegrative.

GAMMA, the third phase, thus seems indicated, but being in the future, must be treated as only prospectively probable.

AREAS AND SUBAREAS

A. Italy. Dominant in the Roman (Gamma) phase of the previous Classical civilization, Italy maintained the strongest transitions between the two cultures; yet, perhaps for that reason, remained relatively non-creative in the High Mediaeval (Alpha) phase of Western, although initiating its Beta phase with the Renaissance. This was perhaps in part due to more retention of cities in Italy, leading in Mediaeval times to city-state republics. Two subareas may have to be recognized in Italy, Northern and Southern. South Italy showed little creative participation until the second half of Beta phase (post-Renaissance).

B. France. Focal in High Mediaeval phase, important in Modern. In some regards, three subareas are significant: Provence, influential in early High Mediaeval times only; Burgundy, chiefly in Late Mediaeval, perhaps through connection with Low Countries; and (Central) France, with focus in Ile de France, throughout.

C. Iberia. Crystallized into Portugal, Spain, and Catalonia. Islamic culture covered most of Iberia in the Pre-Alpha phase, was in slow retreat through most of the High Mediaeval period, but from then on only remnants lingered until near the end of the Late Middle Ages.

D. Low Countries. Belgium and Holland, divided in speech between Romanic and Germanic. Central in the Carolingian empire, with relations (Lotharingia) S as far as Lombardy, expressed in successful early urbanization, with a flowering in Late Mediaeval (Belgium) and early Modern times (Holland).

E. Germany, Austria. Politically retarded through lack of organization—nominal emperor, no strong kings—until XIX C; nationalism long without political expression. Culturally part of Western Europe, but usually with some retardation, especially in manners and taste, punctuated by occasional creativities. Such florescences are: 1, Othonian art, origin not clear, lower Saxony, XI C. 2, Hohenstaufen poetry, climax

1190–1230, on both native and French themes; followed 1230–60 by French-derived Gothic sculpture. 3, Metallurgical and technological inventions, 1150–1550, culminating in printing. 4, Florescence in philosophy, literature, music, 1750–1850, and, diffusely but massively, in science after 1800.

F. West Slavs: Czecho-slovaks and Poles; South Slavs divided between Roman and Byzantine influences. After a IX C attempt at a Great Moravia, the Czechs became, somewhat unwillingly, part of the Roman Empire of the Germans and its culture. Poland resisted German encroachment, and on union with Lithuania became politically successful but culturally marginal to Western Europe, adhering to Rome in religion and script.

G. Scandinavia entered West European civilization 950–1150 with introduction of Christianity and kingship. With this late start, remoteness, and limited resources, it remained retarded, though never wavering in participation. Iceland in its isolation managed a remarkable provincial florescence of a culture retaining native old Norse strains for three centuries after Christianization around 1000. This pre-Occidental Norse or Viking culture had its own florescence 750–1000, and is discussed below (No. 5).

H. Great Britain and Ireland. The southern portions were Megalithic if we accept such a civilization as a genuinely separate one, and after that Keltic, and then Graeco-Roman. The penetration of Roman culture was less deep than in France: Ireland and northern Scotland were never occupied and Britain itself was independent from 286 to 296. Between 383 and 407 Rome withdrew. Within a half-century, Angles and Saxons invaded systematically, slowly subduing the Christianized and the still pagan Kelts (Welsh). The Anglo-Saxons were Christianized from Rome, via Kent and Canterbury, during VII C, in which also the independent Irish Christian church accepted Papal control. Unified English and Scottish kingdoms were achieved early in IX C, but were followed by Danish invasion and conquest, and then by Norman. Beginning with the Norman dynasty and its continental possessions, England entered more fully than before into the rapidly developing French-centered Western civilization, but the rate of participation was uneven: extremely rapid in Norman and Gothic architecture, much slower and weaker in sculpture and literature. Cultural dependence on France continued during the XIV–XV C period of military aggression by smaller but more compact England. Italian influence came later, XVI C, with a temporary revival of French in late XVII. With XVIII C, England perhaps had the higher average standard of living with an effective concentration of wealth, and c. 1750 initiated the Industrial Revolution. The novel and advanced English political institutions were probably related to the economic prosperity both as cause and effect. From XVIII C on, England acknowledged cultural dependence in no field of consequence.

Scotland and Ireland, peripheral by an additional step, lagged correspondingly behind England culturally (as N and W England lagged behind SE), with brief exceptions: namely, Ireland in V–VIII C, the post-Roman, pre-Viking lull, when Britain sheltered the western island from Anglo-Saxon heathenism and turmoil (Toynbee's "Far Western Christian Civilization"); and Scotland, since the voluntary union with England in 1707, which was followed by economic and creative florescence.

I. Russia. The Ukraine entered documented history with the Scythians, –VIII to –II C; Great Russia, with the Scandinavian Varangian dynasty, mid IX C. Christianity and writing came from Constantinople, the former beginning late X C. The large, rather empty country, with trade chiefly in furs and slaves, was remote from higher centers, and its culture grew slowly. Mongol domination from XIII to XV C delayed development of Russian civilization and added little of its own. A strong state formed around Moscow, which expanded toward both the Baltic and Caspian seas and, from 1582 on, into Siberia. The fall of Constantinople to the Turks left the Russians with an independent Greek Orthodox Christianity (with their own patriarch at Moscow since 1589), and a civilization historically tinged rather than effectively molded by Byzantium. The Orthodox and Cyrillic forms of Russian culture however helped to shield it from overly rapid and possibly destructive influencing from the West. Neither the Italian Renaissance nor the Reformation seriously affected Russia. Printing took a century to reach Moscow (1552) from the Rhine. However, technological innovations of consequence kept penetrating; it was the *style* of the West that the Byzantine inheritance succeeded so long in keeping out.

Economic, military, and other practical adoptions were mainly from adjacent Poland and Germany; French influence affected the court, manners, and literature. The Russians were aware of the many superiorities of "European" civilization, and in general were ready to adopt the body of it provided they might give it an autonomous Russian dress or form. Their XIX C impressive florescences in literature and music are European-derived and constitute an integral part of Occidental civilization, but as a characteristic Russian variant of freshness and originality.

Not only Marxism but the revolutionary attitude are imports from the West, made over somewhat to suit specific Russian needs of political control and economic development. Both Russia and the United States are historically derivative from West European culture, and about equally so, but on opposite sides geographically, and with different specialization in interests, direction, and tempo. Both were empty countries that could be and were developed rapidly, uniformly, and effectually in wealth and power. They therefore emerged in 1945 far stronger than the Europe from which they derived but whose competitive development was hindered or slowed in innumerable respects by its own history, by entanglement in the development already achieved.

There are many indications that Western and Central Europe have already begun to alter somewhat their manners and intellectual and aesthetic activities to conform to American or Russian ones, in line with the shift of wealth and power, even though at present neither Russia nor America is yet sufficiently mature to assume intrinsic creative leadership at a good many points.

More or less Russian culture, some adopted, some imposed, has penetrated to many East Russian and Siberian peoples, both in Imperial and in Soviet times, and the process is increasing in tempo. The extension has been overland.

J. Hungary to Turkey. Part of this area is Roman in script and religion, part Greek-Cyrillic and Orthodox. Byzantine civilization being extinct, southeast Europe is now part of Western civilization, but largely by reentry after varying centuries of domination by Islamic Turks. The reentry was partly into the Western political sphere, partly into the Russian, though Yugoslavia has the one openly dissident orbit in that sphere. There is much diversity of speech in the area, though recently somewhat reduced by nationalist pressures and realignments. The same holds for religion: Yugoslavs are divided between Catholic, Orthodox, and Mohammedan. I have already considered and decided against the idea that the culture of the modern Greeks should be considered, like their speech, a perduring survival of ancient Hellenic civilization, though the notion might be maintained. The Turks, when finally stripped of their domination over other peoples, and once more cohesively national, decisively reoriented themselves toward acceptance of Western civilization, including adoption of Roman script and Western calendar, dress, and many institutions, and therewith divested themselves of most of the trappings with which Islam has generally been successful in investing the culture of Mohammedanized peoples. The Turks were aided in accomplishing this break by being relative latecomers in Islam, through having received Islamic culture primarily in its somewhat aberrant Iranic faciēs, and by a Turk-Arab antipathy of long standing. So sharp a turn as they succeeded in making would be much more difficult for Arabic peoples to achieve, because it would involve the tearing out of the very taproots of their culture.

High culture in the area for four thousand years has been centered on the Aegean sea. Inner Thrace, Epirus, and Illyria long remained barbarian and semi-barbarous. Even ancient Macedon almost fronted on the Aegean—a sub-Hellenic district retarded enough to have retained its kingship until Hellenized, whereupon it was able to use its political concentration to overcome the ever-warring Greek cities and, with their reluctant backing, lead the way to the conquest of the top-heavy empire of Persia, and therewith Hellenization for centuries of the upper strata of the Near East. The Illyrian region, roughly Yugoslavia, became important late, as a mainstay of preservation of shaken Roman power and later of its partial restoration under great emperors like Diocletian, Constantine, and Justinian.

K. Ovearseas extensions of Western civilization by emigration from western Europe or conquests by its peoples. "Colonialism" is an unsatisfactory term because it covers two different processes with many grades of transition. The one extreme is instanced by the United States and Australasia, where the significant factor was the settlement by the immigrants, a thinly sown native population of retarded culture being displaced, absorbed, or segregated. The other extreme is India, where a very dense population with an old civilization came to be ruled by a minute number of Europeans. Since 1776 there has been a consistent drift toward political independence of both the overseas emigrant and the conquered populations, beginning with those in which settlement had been the dominant motive. The extension of control over settled native populations that usually grew in size while politically dependent, and that kept their own speech and culture, on the whole came later, in fact largely occurred after the process of immigrant populations achieving their independence was under way or even consummated.

Some of the intermediate situations are: (1) in Mexico, Guatemala, Ecuador, Peru, Bolivia, good-sized native populations were conquered and preserved to be exploited, but these countries achieved national independence as racially mixed populations of Western culture; (2) in South Africa, the native population remains heavily in majority but segregated and without power; (3) in the West Indies, especially the island of Haiti, imported African slaves have largely replaced both the former conquered and conquering populations, with the culture a somewhat incomplete version of West European.

Without exception, every colonialized area has accepted much Western culture. Many are still Westernizing while achieving or developing their independent national fabric. To date, the greatest retentions of native pre-European culture seem likely to be maintained by large and long-civilized peoples like Indians, Indonesians, the Arabic nations.

[†3. MEGALITHIC]

I do not consider as a full civilization the presumably sea-borne Megalithic culture of the west European coasts from Portugal to Denmark, with monumental efflorescences in Brittany and at Stonehenge. Rather, it appears to be an isolable strand in the widely diffused Neolithic-Bronze period culture.

I list the bracketed name mainly in order to have a place open if in the future it should seem that Neolithic-Bronze age Europe ever did develop an important autonomous culture built upon but not wholly derivative from the Near East.

†4. KELTIC

This head is introduced as much to allow brief discussion of two claimants to "civilizationship" as to press for either claim. The two are the Keltic expansion of late pre-Christian centuries and the early Christian Irish development which Toynbee has made into one of his three abortive Civilizations among his twenty-nine, namely, the Far Western Christian.

The Kelts as a branch of the Indo-European peoples never developed anything coherent or developed enough to merit the name of a full civilization. As long as they have been ethnically identifiable, they were on the fringes of higher civilization; or rather just outside and occasionally irrupting in. They formed no durable states, they mostly did without writing. They had sizable towns, but were constituted into oligarchically ruled tribes rather than in city-states or permanent kingdoms. Much of their higher culture was derivative; without the influence of the Greek colony of Massilia, the Gauls of France would have been considerably more retarded than Caesar found them. Yet the LaTène iron culture is considered a distinctively Keltic one, and the preceding one of Hallstadt in central Europe was probably carried in part by Kelts. As for carts and wagons, they seem to have given the Romans not only names but knowledge of kinds of vehicles. Their iron swords carried them to Rome in —IV C, to Delphi and central Anatolian Galatia in —III. Trans-Pyrenaean and trans-Carpathian Galicia are both named after them. They were a vigorous nationality with an expansive phase, but they were as uncoordinated in their culture as undirected in their actions. They constituted ethnographic material of a rather advanced order, but they evolved no organization or discipline sufficient for an autochthonous civilization or a distinctive facies of one. The avidity with which they took on Roman civilization in Gaul once they were pacified argues how much less culture of their own they possessed.

As for the early Irish, Toynbee's own enthusiastic rating carries some conviction; yet it is difficult to pin-point many accomplishments. They became voluntary Christians about or just after the time Rome was withdrawing from Great Britain, learning it from Romanized Britons rather than from Rome, so the conversion was unaccompanied by political presence, nor was it followed by new super-kingships as among Germans, Scandinavians, and Slavs. The culture which St. Patrick found in V C Ireland was a belated Indo-European one of Homeric and Rig-Vedic type, with war chariots, heroes, cattle lifting, slaves, endless fighting and boasting—and with an oral mythology and literature about such doings. What is most surprising is that this old life and the new Christianity got on well together and throve; perhaps because in Ireland they were beyond dependable reach of popes, church councils, Rome, or Constantinople. Quite possibly the writing which the missionaries brought in and the native monks cultivated was felt as a technical aid by the poets. The Irish monks retransferred their version of Christianity to Britons and Saxons in Scotland and England before Roman missionaries arrived. But before long the greater world prevailed, and in VII C the Irish church accepted the Papacy. The Irish literature seems to have continued for some centuries, still feeding on native themes, though long since deprived of its taproot of autochthonous religion. If we knew the dates of composition instead of the dates of manuscripts, a climax would probably be evident in this literature. It perhaps manifested more imagination though less control than Norse.

The Irish never achieved serious political consolidation or military expansion. Along with Scotland they were exposed to the earliest Viking raids, and in the early IX century were Norse-dominated. Very little of Mediterranean civilization ever reached Ireland, other than Christianity and letters, and while Western civilization finally absorbed the Irish one because of much greater massiveness, it was still struggling to take form when the Irish one had probably passed its peak.

†5. NORSE OR VIKING CIVILIZATION

The case is somewhat better for Norse than for Irish culture being accorded full status as a minor or "abortive" civilization just outside the main ecumenical stream, as Toynbee has done. In *Configurations*, 1944 (pp. 590–594, 727, 732–734) I substantially though not formally recognized it as such. The arguments for a distinctive Norse civilization are several.

1. The astounding aggressive and expansive Viking energy, sometimes backed by skillful political organization, as in Normandy, Sicily, Russia.

2. A narrow but highly stylized literature, rooted in a non-Christian pagan mythology, and wholly autonomous in formal means as well as themes.[1] This achievement of highly wrought form in the lone cultural field of poetry is shared with the Irish culture, and is strangely reminiscent of the pre-Islamic Arabs, who further resembled the Vikings in successful aggressiveness.

3. After Christianization, the Norsemen in remote Iceland, where they were somewhat protected against too rapid flattening out of their cultural peculiarities by the growing mass of Western civilization, continued their literature with change of theme and manner for about three centuries. They wrote Christian poems in alliterative style. Panegyric or sometimes historical poems by skalds took the place of mythological and heroic ones. The skaldic forms were basically Eddaic, but stricter and more elaborate, and with more extravagant metaphors and beginnings of internal rhyme and count of syllables, although European-style end rhymes come in only in mid-XIV C. Most significant of all was the development of an effective true prose style employed in biographic sagas which came close to being novels and evinced extraordinary psychological insight and emotional restraint; and alongside these, genuine histories were written. Sarton in his comparative *History of Science*, volume 2, 1931, is eloquent and concise

1. Some of the final Norse attainments, like the Voluspo in the Poetic Edda, may have been fostered by the stimulus of contact with Western civilization, without being derivative.

about this intellectual-aesthetic florescence in isolated Iceland while mainland Scandinavia was humbly entering the primary class in the school of European civilization.

One could not hope that a culture of the limited scope of the Norse would survive once it came into contact with Western civilization, though isolation might delay its extinction. The greater civilization had too many inheritances drained into it: Christianity, with its Hebrew root; the Roman Empire, heir itself to Hellenism; besides all the earlier more oriental cultures that had flowed into this. But the Norsemen originated, and partly salvaged from their barbarian Germanic antecedents, enough values independent of the main stream to warrant their culture being recognized as a notably distinctive one of the second rank. In this point I am confident that we must accept the judgment of Toynbee.

If I hesitate rather more to put the Irish culture quite on the same level, it is for several reasons. (1) It was earlier and its society was crushed earlier—by Vikings, Normans, and English. (2) It was Christianized six hundred years earlier, and while the Christianization was friendlier and perhaps even stimulative, it must also have helped in time to deliver Irish culture over to the encroaching Occident. (3) The configuration of original Irish literature makes much less of an intelligible pattern than Norse literature. Its presentation has been more in terms of Irish patriotism than as a time-oriented development, with the result that it emerges historically nearly flat. This may be the outcome of historic accidents: themes originating before Christianization, but preserved and perhaps much developed with the writing that Christianity brought in (V-VIII C), then the Viking destruction, and, as a result, preserved manuscripts beginning only in XI C, with literary activity still going on, though evidently much modified. The result is that the pattern of the literature's growth is palimpsested instead of clear. The two literatures have much in common in general habitus, in native subject and form, and through contacts, but there is great need of a sober, orderly, developmental account of the Irish one, because culture-historical understanding of old Irish culture must depend largely on the native literature that has been preserved.

[6. RUSSIA]

I have already set forth above why the civilization of Russia should be considered in the main a variant facies, by gradual assimilation, of European and Western civilization, in spite of a degree of early distinctness due to remoteness, further differentiated by a stream of Byzantine influencing.

We are likely to overlook the close relationship of Russian culture to our own because of the current tensions between them, forgetting that such tensions are acute precisely because the two sociocultural aggregates are similar enough to engage in consistent rivalry.

It is however only fair to recall that the pan-Slavist philosopher of history Danilevsky believed that Russian culture was a distinct "type" that would supercede European; that Spengler, while not formally listing it because he considered it as still only formative, did admit it as a probable monadal entity of the future; and that Toynbee recognizes an Orthodox Christian Russian Offshoot civilization beginning in IX C, with the Muscovite empire as its universal state and its universal peace ending in 1881. Spengler construed the Europeanization of Russia as misdirected and vain, and as destined to fail because contrary to its inherent nature. He saw the characterizing symbol of Russia in the endless plain of brotherhood, and its inner spirit in humble, anonymous Christianity. I hold with none of these opinions.

AREAL DELIMITATIONS OF WESTERN CIVILIZATION

[This is a further expansion of the ideas which Kroeber indicated in the preceding outline of a roster of European Civilizations, sections 4, 5, and 6.]

THE NORSE CULTURE

LET us now attempt the areal delimitation of Western civilization. This is the equivalent of deciding which neighboring societies with their cultures are to be included in or excluded from the Western civilization. The societies in question are the Norse, Irish, Byzantine, and Russian. Others are too remote in time or place to come into consideration; or, like Islam, too competitively set off in dominant religion and in cultural language.

The Irish and the Norse civilizations were first listed as independent units, in the comparative study of civilizations, by Toynbee. Of the two, I have substantially recognized the Norse as independent;[1] though my approach, which proceeded piecemeal by type of cultural activities rather than by civilizational unit, conceded the independence incidentally rather than emphasizing it.

At any rate, there are several reasons for considering early Norse culture as a unit possessing more properties distinctive of itself than shared with Western culture. These reasons are: First, the astounding expansive energy of the society in the Viking period. The success of this expansion was certainly not due to numbers and can hardly be attributed altogether to superior "daring" and "bravery." There

1. Configurations, 590–594, 727, 732–734, 1944.

must have been techniques and attitudes, in other words cultural patterns of organizing the expansive energy, to make it successful. There were also evident aptitudes, resting on just what antecedents we do not know, for political organization; as manifested in Normandy, Sicily, Kiev. There was finally a narrow but highly stylized and original literature which was rooted in a non-Christian pagan religion, as the whole Viking-Norse culture was autonomously pagan.[2] And the forms and sentiments of this literature were wholly diverse from those of Classical, Christian, or Western literatures.[3] All in all, these are sufficient grounds for construing Norse culture as independent, and as parallel to the then formative Western civilization. It constituted a smaller but autonomous growth. It succumbed because of its historic isolation and consequent quantitative meagerness of cultural content. Western civilization was reinforced and enriched by the heritage of Christianity and the residues of Classical civilization that entered into its very formation. It was thus bound to win over Early Scandinavian culture by sheer mass and compass. But this fact does not detract from the vigorous originality of the Norse growth; and around 900 the outcome of the competition might still have seemed dubious to contemporaries.

IRISH RELATION TO THE WEST

In contrast with Norse, the Irish culture, which Toynbee has depicted so glowingly, under the title of the Far Western Christian civilization, can be credited with only a minor degree of native originality. It is basically Christian; though it is remarkable for being a Christian culture in an area to which Rome had not penetrated, and

2. Some of the final Norse attainments may have been fostered by the stimulus of clash with Western culture, without the attainments however being in any sense derivative. Compare the Voluspo.

3. This notable achievement of a highly wrought form in the single cultural field of poetry—in addition to war, pillage, and government—is strangely reminiscent of the pre-Islamic Arabs.

which had formed before Western civilization had begun to form. It is in these facts, and in its extreme areal marginality, that the peculiar quality and poignancy of the old Irish culture lie. Where Norse culture was once a fighting competitor of our own, the Irish was, in its own orientation, a sort of friendly predecessor that paved the way. Like Nubia and then Abyssinia, beyond Egypt and then Rome, Ireland also lay beyond the frontiers and remained largely outside the civilized Oikoumenê, though it became Christian early. In a sense, the native Irish culture ended with the loss of autonomy by the early Irish church. Its outstanding thinker, ninth-century Erigena, was drawn to the mainland to bolster the Carolingian "renaissance." Irish Gaelic literature continued for centuries, feeding on native themes, though long since deprived of its taproot of autochthonous religion. It manifested probably more creative imagination than Norse, but less control. There never was a notable expansion of the society: the Irish tended to waste themselves in intertribal bickerings. As a successful autonomous growth, native Irish culture ended on the whole earlier than Norse. On the other hand Irishmen began to produce creatively within European civilization barely four centuries ago. This was, as might be expected, by way of England; but as it was also by participation in Protestant English literature, it indicated that independent Irish culture, which was Catholic and Gaelic, was long dead as a growth.

In fine, the imported element was perhaps not much larger in the old Irish civilization than in Norse; but the native ingredient lacked expansiveness, and its growth therefore remained restricted and terminated earlier. We cannot fairly relegate the Irish culture to being a sub-unit of Western civilization, because both its formation and such culmination as it attained preceded the definitive crystallizing out of Western civilization. It was thus a sort of remote, precocious, short-lived older half-sister of our own civilization; whereas the Norse was no kin at all, and tended to remain hostile or exploitive. Toynbee is right in wholly separating off the Irish from Western civilization. But it began too early at a far edge, with too undeveloped a culture of its own and too little of the Classical heritage ever to be able to grow much internally or externally. With its situation, it was therefore almost bound to be absorbed in Western civilization when this gradually grew and expanded. Toynbee's designation of the Irish as an abortive civilization is therefore appropriate. It was like a seed that germinated early in thin soil near a more richly nurtured competitor.

BYZANTINE RELATION TO THE WEST

Byzantine civilization is most simply construed as a prolongation of Graeco-Roman. It persisted into much later times and therefore into very different sociocultural environments, which increasingly modified it. Such seems to be the usual classification of it by historians. Toynbee calls the Byzantine civilization Orthodox Christian, and sees it affiliated to the Hellenic civilization through a chrysalis church of alien origin, namely Christianity. In this is resembles Western civilization: the two are evidently twin sisters. Spengler, Danilevsky, Petrie, Northrop essentially ignore Byzantium as a major civilization.

Politically, the Byzantine empire was a continuation of the Roman. The main capital was shifted in 330 from Rome to Constantinople to be nearer the empire's center of population, wealth, cultivation, and defensibility against aggression. But the city was long called New Rome, the empire remained the Roman empire, and in the sixth century it reconquered from Germanic barbarian invaders considerable parts of Italy, Spain, and Africa. The inhabitants called themselves Romans; the ethnic Greeks retained this name until well into the nineteenth century. Modern Rumania, Roumelia, and the mediaeval Turkish kingdom of Rum in Anatolia express the same continuity.

Ethnically—that is, linguistically—Greek always was the administrative as well as cultural language of the eastern half of the Roman empire. When the western half crumbled away, Greek soon became the residual official speech of the empire, and the vernacular of large tracts in it. Latin was maintained for a few centuries as the language of jurisprudence and perhaps of military command. Justinian's Institutes and Digest were still compiled in Latin, though before long translated into Greek. Ancient Greek remained more or less intelligible until about a thousand years ago. And even today it is apparently nearer to spoken Greek than Latin is to Italian. Homer remained the great poet all through Byzantine history.

Geographically a similar continuity was maintained. For several centuries the empire consisted of the lands that Alexander the Great overran—or, more exactly, those that his Greek-speaking and Greek-thinking successors maintained after about −250: namely Alexander's conquests without Iran and Irak. When the New Islamic storm subsided, Syria, Palestine, Egypt, North Africa had been torn away, and their upper classes soon learned to speak Arabic instead of Greek. About half the original Byzantine empire remained: the peninsula of Asia Minor and that of the Balkans, enclosing between them the Aegean sea, the immemorial home of the Hellenes and even of their Minoan-Mycenaean predecessors.

Only in religion was there a break with the past. And even this was a break only with the remoter past of Hellenic culmination; not with the immediate past of joint Graeco-Latin empire under Roman domination, which had become Christian before the Greek East and the Latin West gradually broke apart.

It is evidently only because Toynbee accords primacy to the religious factor wherever he can, that he constitutes the Byzantine empire into a separate civilization, the Orthodox Christian. If the Christian Latin West grew into the Catholic civilization which we call Western, the Christian Greek East of the former empire can be regarded as growing into the Orthodox civilization—so his tacit argument appears to run. And it is sound enough if religion is to be singled out as the decisive determinant of cultural autonomy.

If however we prefer to admit multiple factors as being determinative, the political, linguistic, geographic, and general continuities with the past outweigh the change in religion. Byzantine or Orthodox civilization is in that case most simply construed as a final phase of Graeco-Roman; marked off as a phase by its unchallenged and dominant Christianity.

Among cultural traits that are symptomatic of this continuance are the circus. Christianity suppressed the gladiatorial shows in West and

East alike. But the chariot races and even their blue and green factions went on in Constantinople for many centuries after their institution in early Imperial Rome. Literature continued not only with the standards of appreciation of pagan days but for long largely with the same meters and forms. We have already spoken of the final codification of Roman law under Justinian—himself an Illyrian Latin—three centuries or more after the great basic jurists—most of them Greek-speaking Asiatics—had written the basic treatises.

On the other side, as the West crumbled away and barbarized, the Greek Byzantines were more exclusively thrown upon Eastern contacts: and these left many influences. Spengler has called Diocletian the first Khalif, and St. Sophia a Christian cupola mosque of Asiatic type. It is certainly true that from Constantine on the Byzantine emperors were "autocrators," monarchs as unlimited as any Asiatic despots, ancient or modern. The old Greek and Italic city-state was gone, after having survived, as a form of local communal government, through three centuries of Roman empire. Architecture, even if Spengler exaggerated the fact, certainly assimilated some eastern forms; and the thoroughly non-Greek, non-concrete direction of Byzantine mosaic and eikon art is notorious. This art is symbolic and ideational, where Hellenic sculpture and painting were sensate and representative in bent. Byzantine art is most familiar to us from Ravenna, the center and rivet of Byzantine hold and influence in Italy. The great eighth-century surge of Iconoclasm is the ideological expression of the same trend. It was a puritanical reform as definitely hostile to even suggestions of idols as was Mohammedanism; if indeed the movement was not stimulated within Christian Orthodoxy by the example of nearby Mohammedan fervor. Eunuchism, which the rest of Christianity refused to tolerate, won long acceptance in the Orientalized court of Constantinople. While the West substituted feudalism for government, Byzantium was administered by a civilian bureaucracy that was efficient if grinding, and had counterparts—at least temporary ones—in the Khalifate, India, and China.

These eastern relations can also be seen, in wider perspective, as continuations of Hellenic times. After a century and a half of uneasy Greek-Asiatic equilibrium following Marathon, Alexander overran the

Near East, and left Hellenic rule and Hellenic culture established there. The political dominance had become feeble when the Romans took over—Bactria, Persia, Mesopotamia, even Palestine and Galatia, had broken from Greek rule. But Greek culture was firmly established on the upper levels of society. And since Roman upper-level culture was similarly derived from Greek, the Romans, in taking over the government of Hellenistic Asia and Egypt, supported and froze the Hellenistic culture there also. In doing this they quite likely perpetuated for long centuries what without their interference might have melted away sooner. The reconstruction of a zealot Jewish state, then of the great Sassanian Persian empire, Zenobia's Arab attempt and the subsequent lightning-like triumphs of Islam—all these indicate that Greek culture had never become rooted all the way through Near Eastern society. The lower classes, especially where they preserved their vernaculars, remained anti-Greek, Asiatic, "Magian," in various degrees. If so, an anti-Hellenic reaction was due—ultimately extending perhaps even to an Asianization of the Greek homeland. The Romans not only delayed this return swing of influence, but moderated its force when it arrived. It came therefore only in Byzantine times, and without overwhelming strength. But the Asian pendulum did swing back; and its effects are part of what characterized Byzantine culture as Byzantine and enabled it to drift so far apart from the Christian West as it did.

This last is the summary of a construal—a "theory," social "scientists" would call it—and is submitted as such. Though it may be added that all historic interpretation consists of construals, and the ultimate possible judgment of them occurs through appraisal of greater or less pattern coherence in the total context of the data and their interpretation.

RUSSIAN RELATION TO THE WEST

The separateness of Russian civilization from Western is admitted not only by Danilevsky, the pan-Slavic bias of whose theorizing demands such independence, but by Spengler and Toynbee. But these two last differ radically in their depiction of the historic course of the civilization.

Toynbee sees Russian civilization (which he calls the "Orthodox Christian Offshoot in Russia") forming in the tenth century—presumably with the acceptance of Christianity in 988 by the Scandinavian-ruled Slavs under Vladimir. He puts Russia's Time of Troubles[1] from 1075 to 1478, and her Universal State from 1478 to 1881. These two continuous periods of four centuries each absorb, between them, most of the history of the Russian civilization. The date 1075 represents [the disintegration of Kievan Russia]; 1478 (1480) marks the end of Mongol Tatar overlordship under Ivan the Great; 1881, the assassination of Alexander II. The time since 1881 presumably falls into the Toynbeean period of "Successor States"—at any rate into the general phase of disintegration. It would be marked by the war with Japan and the consequent attempted revolution, by the participation in World War I and collapse, by the civil wars and the Bolshevik taking over.

This seems a somewhat unfortunate interpretation of Russian history. The formative pre-Troubles period is too short: only a tenth of the total duration of the civilization. It also has too little cultural content. As a civilization, Russia in 1075 had accomplished very little. Something of a sense of nationality had emerged and had found expression in a loose, rude political fabric and in well-established Christianity. But technology, the arts, economics, law, and literacy and competence generally were still tremendously backward: not only as compared with Constantinople but with say contemporary France. And of any conscious independent intellectual or aesthetic effort there was scarcely a trace. To see the next eight centuries as the stages in which this barely formed civilization mainly underwent the experiences of teetering in the balance of dissension, and then being frozen into a static empire of power, is disproportionate. Retarded as the Muscovy of Ivan the Great and Ivan the Terrible may have been by western standards,

1. The phrase as here used is Toynbee's technical term for a period of disunity and dissension preceding the Universal State, as a phenomenon tending to recur in all civilizations: for instance, in Chou China, what Chinese historians call the era of Contending States, 479–221, before the unified Empire of Ch'in and Han. This technical term is itself taken from Russian history, there denoting the interdynastic interval 1598–1613, with Boris Godunov, Pseudo-Demetrius, and the Polish occupation. These two senses—Toynbee's generic one and the particular Russian reference—must of course be kept apart.

it possessed more culture, and a more patterned or organized culture, than the Varangian Kiev of Vladimir and Yaroslav. As a civilization as well as a state it was not in breakdown under these Ivans of the fifteenth and sixteenth centuries, but in actual growth. It was at least as successful, and more advanced, than the proto-Russia of 1000. This is a case where Toynbee has perhaps been too intent on his formula. He seems to have thought too narrowly in terms of the society itself, its sociopolitical organization, its accepted religion, and perhaps the moral drives of a few of its leaders, and in so doing has forgotten that the flesh and blood of a civilization is after all a structured body of culture, a corpus of transmitted and further developed culture material.

True, a civilization of course presupposes a society. And we can expect that there will usually be an accepted church, a political fabric, military events, and influential leaders or groups. But these are only the accompanying factors that operate on a civilization and help to shape it. They may more or less depict its narrowly historical fortunes, the course of certain outward events connected with it. They do not describe the civilization, nor even recognize its particular characteristics. And they are certainly not a substitute for a history of the civilization itself—for the story of the course which its culture ran. Toynbee's interpretation of Russia too largely leaves out Russian civilization in the endeavor to fit events to a schema.

Spengler's interpretation of Russia is wholly different. It agrees with Toynbee's—and Danilevsky's—only on the one point that Russia does not form part of Western civilization. To Spengler, Russian culture is possibly, or might have been, of the future: at any rate, it has not yet really emerged. Its prodromal, unconscious stage, corresponding to that of the Merovingians in the West (481–687), Spengler puts in the time between the emancipation from Tatar domination in 1480 and Peter the Great's founding of St. Petersburg in 1703.[2] Peter's westernization is to Spengler a second instance of his process of "pseudomorphosis," by which the earlier nascent Magian culture of the Near East had been forced into the foreign and uncongenial world of Hellenism. Peter and his successors forced Russia successively into

2. 2:192. The respective stages thus lasted 206 years for the Franks and 223 years in Russia.

Baroque, Enlightened, and nineteenth-century forms, he says. Tolstoy is the exponent and victim of this "Petrinization": he is half Western, half Russian, rebelling against the West but made of it, speaking of Christ but thinking like Marx. The truly Russian attitude, according to Spengler, is represented by Dostoyevsky—to whose primitive kind of Christianity the next millennium will belong.[3] Bolshevism is the "lees" of the Western infiltration within which a third type of Christianity, a priestless type, is forming, much more similar to the Magian than to the Western Faustian expression of Christianity; and this new Christianity will in time blot out from Russia even the memory of machine industry and money.[4]

This is prophecy, and there is no reasoning with proofs and argument against inspiration, least of all when the seer knows the innermost soul of a people and culture. But it is clear that Spengler does not recognize a Russian culture that has already had its career or most of it. He does recognize something that is struggling to express itself historically as a distinctive and unique Russian culture, but which so far has been cramped and smothered by influences from the neighboring, mature, and far more advanced culture of Western Europe. With this we can fully agree. When Spengler goes on from this to predict that the centuries of assimilation to the West will fail in spite of the successes of the Western-derived Communist regime—because of them, indeed—we can part company with him and let him go his way. But his insistence that in its historic origins Russia is a growth mainly separate from Western Europe, every historian will agree to. And that its Westernization in the past three centuries, its pseudomorphosis, has produced strange inconsistencies and strong internal strains, of which the successful Bolshevization is one product—this any anthropologist would recognize as an example of "acculturation" or large-scale intercultural influencing in the direction of assimilation. That the Old Russian "soul" will ultimately break through again and cause life in Russia to revert to a sort of rural Christianity of universally levelled brotherhood and suffused peasant obscurity—well, possibly so; but it is hardly a point that can be argued with evidence at present; and

3. 2:196.

4. 2:495, 504.

when it comes to guessing, probably most of us would not bet on the reversion but against it.

We have here, then, two opposite views. Toynbee credits Russia with a civilization which constitutes one of several Christian branches, but which has ever been of modest cultural attainments and is apparently finished. Danilevsky and Spengler see Russian civilization as of the future, as not yet fully achieved. But they differ among themselves in that Danilevsky regards the nineteenth-century attainments of Russia as an earnest of greater achievements to come; Spengler, as something forced on Russia which she will rebelliously expel in order to revert to a wholly different and presumably rudimentary culture. This clash of views—even if we disregard their predictional parts—shows how little "reliability" we have as yet attained in the comparative study of civilizations.

My analysis of Russian florescences in science, literature, and music shows that these correspond closely in time and in manner of relationship to the nineteenth-century participations in western culture of other marginal countries: Poland, Scandinavia, America.[5] All these florescences were induced and definitely derivative, though at times with a considerable national flavoring, this last especially in Russia.

Going back once more in time, we can agree with Toynbee that a potential civilization started to grow in Russia before the year 1000, with the emergence of a national sense transcending tribal limits and with the acceptance of Christianity. This new religion brought with it certain strongly associated elements, such as a degree of literacy, kingship, regulated international relations, perhaps coinage. As a result of geography, this cultural import reached the Russian tribes from Constantinople instead of Rome, and with Greek instead of Latin antecedents. However, as we have already shown, the Russian event was the close counterpart, in its nature as well as in its time, of events among the western Slavs, in Hungary, in Scandinavia, and in Britain. In all these marginal areas, parallel phenomena occurred around 1000 in which Christianization was associated with remanifestations of institutions and culture that had previously been established on the Mediterranean.

5. Configurations, 728, 730–732; also 164, 603–606, 653–654.

The difference between Russia and the other marginal incipient cultures of the period of 1000 was that these others surrounded a hearth in western Europe, with its focus especially in France, in which the creatively productive Western civilization was developing. In this new civilization the marginal European nations were not able to participate very actively; but most of them did participate passively or receptively, and then sometimes derivatively. But from this process of centuries Russia was as good as excluded: partly by her first Byzantine conditionings, then by the atrophy of Byzantium and by the growing aloofness of Constantinople and the West. The consequence was that Russia alone remained untouched by the great cultural events of the High Mediaeval West. Gothic architecture and sculpture, stained glass windows, vernacular poetries, Scholastic philosophy, new monastic currents, Feudalism, the Crusades—all passed her by. In contrast, even distant Scotland, Norway, Poland, and Hungary were caught somewhat in the swirl. By say 1150 this great swell was in full surge in the West, while in Russian lands culture stood still and political redisintegration had set in. A century later, just about as the West was reaching its Mediaeval climax, the destructive Mongol storm burst on Russia.

The consequence in turn of all this was that when around 1480 Russia had at last achieved essential political reintegration[6] and unification, she was centuries behind Europe. In the West, by then, the Italian Renaissance had risen almost to the level at which it was to flood Europe. The Netherlands prospered in manufactures, music, and painting. Portugal was well on the way to the Cape and India, Spain but a decade from America. Printing had been discovered in Germany a generation before—it reached Moscow only in 1552—and the Reformation lay around the corner of the century. As against this Russia had nothing to show except a healthily successful nationalism and institutions of a rugged if semibarbarous character.

Meanwhile Constantinople was gone, Arab civilization long since spent as a force, the leadership of Islam fallen into the hands of the also semibarbarous Osmanli Turks. Thus Russia around 1500 not only possessed no oriented culture of her own, but had nowhere to turn

6. Absorptions not yet effectuated in 1480 were: Tver, 1485; trans-Uralic Yugra, 1499; Pskov, 1510; Ryazan, 1517; Chernigov, 1523.

for orientation. But the West passed into the full cultural development of its Modern phase, and expanded geographically eastward as well as west. So, by about 1600, the West began actively impinging on Russia. During the century that followed, Westernization crept more into vogue, and by 1700, under Peter, it came into conscious authority. The native developments in culture were too simple and small when Russia had reattained coherence and independence by 1500, and the century or two thereafter were too short for substantial native achievements to be made before contacts with the West became active. So from 1000/1700 on the far greater mass of Western civilization bore down increasingly on the healthy, tough, but crude, unorganized, and ineffectual Russian culture, and the process of assimilation began. That so much characteristic native physiognomy and function were retained is obviously due to the extent of Russian territory, the size of the population, its continued political independence; in a measure too, probably, to the separateness of the form of Christianity and the alphabet.

Russia in short had by 1917 become assimilated to Western civilization externally and in part internally; what of its culture remained non-Western was rather indistinctive because it had never yet developed patterns that were both purely native and effectively characterized. When the Communists seized control, they deliberately broke up, as thoroughly as they knew how, society and wealth as well as state and church,[7] in order to create a new culture which is intended to supersede Western civilization but whose plan is most evidently a product derivative from that same Western civilization. So far as this new prospective culture is not Western, it is super-Western: a sort of ideological dream, forecasting, or trying to anticipate, the trend of the currents of Western culture.

We thus emerge with a picture of Russia in history different from both Spengler's and Toynbee's, and yet not wholly at variance. One of these two sees Russian civilization lying wholly in the past, the other in the future. We see a history—within about the dates cited by Toynbee—of a nationality slowly forming, ever groping, but hardly achieving

7. Established science and art are at the moment (May 1949) having their turn at the destruction which must precede reconstitution.

a civilization of its own. Russia gave birth to too little culture of distinctive style originality to deserve the term civilization with the same import as western Europe or the Mediterranean. Toynbee sees the Russian culture ending with the breakdown of its empire. I see it essentially absorbed, though as a semi-autonomous and resistive segment, in the still expanding greater civilization which is assimilating it; unless, as Danilevsky visioned it, his Russia is to assimilate the West, to dispossess and inherit it.

With Spengler I share the denial to Russia of a past major civilization of its own. I share also his recognition of Russian national resistance to assimilatory acculturation, in recent centuries as today. And I would agree further in admitting the *possibility* that Russia may yet achieve a distinctive new culture. Only I see this possible new civilization not as a reversion to something ancient, primitive, rural, and mystic, but as a more or less novel and distinctive modification or phase of Western civilization. If, on the contrary, this new Russian development were really to eventuate as simple, folksy, and pious, it would, almost by definition, be not a civilization but one of the Dark Ages of regression between civilizations. And it is difficult to see this as happening in Russia without its happening also in the West: so great have the assimilation and linkage between the two become. Even the tensions of the moment express a struggle that is essentially internal, as between embittered brothers.

MINOR CIVILIZATIONS IN NATIVE NORTH AMERICA

[*This material properly belongs under section 61 of the Substantive Roster, the Southwest (New World).*]

As we shift our regard away from the developed civilizations of Nuclear America as they are characterized by metallurgical arts, by masonry, by cities or states, and in part by a calendar of permutating type, we find that formerly there extended, all the way to the Arctic Ocean, an array of some hundreds of petty nationalities, usually called "tribes," of fairly uniformly lower level of culture as compared with our own, or even with that of the native peoples of the relatively advanced "Nuclear" area. Actually, if we substitute for the ambiguous word "tribe" a definable term, such as "autonomous territory-owning group," the number of socially, politically, and culturally independent units was certainly well over a thousand, north of central Mexico. Obviously, the differences between these in customs could not have been very great nor important as compared with our own civilization.

The tribal differentiation seems to us particularly minute as between units that adjoined or lived near enough together to trade, to practice some intermarriage, occasionally to visit neighboring festivals, and who were thus in position to influence or imitate one another's institutions. Even warfare sets up a relation productive of trends to assimilation at certain points. Where the groups are homebound, averse to shifts into wholly new terrain, and therefore normally sessile for prolonged periods, the differentiation of customs from one to the next group is not only slight but so regular that its degree may be approximately predicted.

Such approximate predictability is particularly striking where its expression is quantitative—in the number of isolable or definable items of culture: "elements" or "traits," they are usually called by anthropologists. For instance in the region of north central California I have estimated[1] that adjacent tribelet groups would share about 95 per cent of the discrete items of their culture or total customs and beliefs. Around four per cent of the culture would be known to two adjacent groups, on the average, but practiced regularly by only one of them —due to lack of natural resources in the territory held, or as customs on the way out but remembered, or one only beginning to be introduced. Trade, or permitted visits, can mitigate deficiencies of natural environment, such as lack of ocean shellfish from the diet of a group living not too far inland. Finally, I estimated that perhaps one per cent of the total enumerable inventory of items in the culture of each group represented peculiarities distinctive of it: innovations not taken up by its neighbors, or not retained.

Of course as one compares the culture of a group with the *second* one beyond it, which is subject to influences from groups at third remove, the proportion of traits distinctive of each grows, the fre-

1. The percentages cited are only exemplary estimates, because technical difficulties still prevent wholly accurate counts. Native informants may misunderstand points inquired into, or happen to be hazy about them in certain ranges—as men about women's occupations and techniques, the fortunate about the makeshifts of the disadvantaged. Or custom may be in process of changing. Ethnographers also can misunderstand, or be insufficiently patient, or have their background knowledge, a measure of which is prerequisite to intelligent inquiry, weighted or colored by previous experience in different regions. At any rate, they inevitably project into the study some measure of personal equation, the varying strengths of which are apparent but difficult to correct for. An ideal comparative element study would put at least two independent inquirers into each native group, each of them working with several informants, then comparing for conflicting entries, and finally returning to the group for resolution of remaining contradictions and ambiguities. All this would be very time-consuming and therefore expensive. The University of California Element Survey of 1934–38 was a pilot study in which thirteen ethnographers collected data from 254 Indian groups in western North America, obtaining altogether half a million cultural items. The interest was comparative and historical, the procedure therefore extensive. Some of the criticism made of the endeavor was that it lacked the intensity of prolonged analytical or functional acquaintance with a single culture, which is of course true, but involves a different objective.

quency of shared ones diminishes; and thus according to number of intervening social units—and, roughly, to distance apart in miles.

Where the social units are more populous than in California, and the areas held by each are larger, the respective percentages of cultural items actually shared, potentially shared or ambiguous, and distinctive, may decrease and increase; but whatever the new ratios, they will tend to be constant in the area being considered.

From all this it may be inferred that culture change over most of North America was gradual and progressive, mainly slow but steady, not often disturbed or hastened by great events. If a tribe was conquered, destroyed or scattered, its social fabric and culture disrupted, it was likely to be by another tribe not too far away and of similar culture; so that the total picture of mode of life in the area a hundred years later would no doubt in consequence have been different in certain details, but little changed as a whole. Fundamental inventions, like agriculture or metallurgy, were of course very rarely made; and above all they were made or adopted piecemeal and gradually. It was in the range and intensity of the practice of farming, or of metal working, that one millennium or region differed effectively from another, not in the fact that the abstract *idea* of planting or smelting had come to be known. This is shown to be true by most of the archaeological record as it has been dug from the ground; also by the many tribes that plant but still also gather and hunt extensively; or who have shifted back and forth into and out of agriculture; or who live with similar institutions side by side, one of them farming and the other one not.

This holds for native times. When Europeans irrupted, with ships and firearms, horses and cattle, new economies and wants—with culture of thoroughly different cast, in short, the consequences were different. The Spaniards tended to subjugate, utilize the native society by incorporation if it was not too resistive, and bracket remains of the native culture into their own. Portuguese, French, British, and Dutch hardly tried to build themselves rich and populous new realms, and long clung to the coast and large rivers, ruining or driving out the native societies that stood in their way. But they also introduced new culture—guns, horses, kettles, needles, money, bounties, the fur trade—which spread faster than they spread, and so altered the customs and living of peoples that had not yet seen a European. This was what generally happened when they obtained a foothold of settlement. The disruptive expedition of de Soto shook the tribes from Georgia to Arkansas, but, melting away itself, left few sure traces a century later of influences on their culture.

Similarly with the ships that must have been blown across the Pacific time and again. They came singly, with small, often famished or resourceless crews. The effects of their landfalls were randomly scattered, became dissipated, were absorbed in the mass of native culture as this was gradually changing from its own inner momentum. There must have been sea-born Asiatic influences on the Pacific coasts; but they are exceedingly hard to trace into any coherent pattern, so that we are still embarrassed to decide whether certain resemblances are fortuitous, independently convergent, or the result of contacts.

All in all, the total picture for North America suggests that its native cultures have been subject to processes operative continuously and steadily, analogous to secular uplift, denudation, and erosion of the earth's crust, rather than to cataclysmic crises and sudden but fundamental innovations. Seen in long historical perspective, native culture does slope upward in time, but gently and evenly. Viewed in momentary cross section, as it first came into the ken of members of Occidental culture, it lay spread out rather evenly, with little of marked contour. It seems almost a still pool, a historyless, unstructured ethnographic reservoir of the sort that Danilevsky and Spengler saw as containing all primitive culture, and from which now and then an organized great civilization somehow emerged.

As I have said before, I do not hold in principle with any distinction of kind between "civilized" and pre-civilized cultures, nor between literate and preliterate, though writing does always add a new factor. To believe that there have been only eight or ten structured and definable cultures or culture-historical types, as Spengler and Danilevsky assert, or twenty-odd as Toynbee enumerates them, seems to me civilizatio-centric, if I may coin an ugly word in extension from ethnocentric. Continuities run not only through each of the great civilizations but also between them, and a dividing of them off from one another is always likely to include an element of the arbitrary or subjective, though this may be covered up by concurrence of usage. In principle it is extremely improbable that advanced cultures contain any quality of structure that is wholly lacking in less developed ones. Such a complete distinction seems as erroneous theoretically as it would be to deny structure to a planarian worm because it lacks certain organs or organ systems that occur in mammals.

What counts in the determination of a culture—high or low—as being well characterized and justifiably segregable in some measure, is not so much its content, most of which is likely to recur in other cultures, but the circumstance by which content has been selected, and especially whether there is visible, some distinctiveness of organization of this content into a coherent pattern or functioning plan.

Within the gently variable continuum in which culture normally extends through area and time, then, there separate out here and there somewhat greater variations comparable to clottings or coagulations in a continuous liquid—to crystallizations, if one will. They are primarily recognizable as special or distinctive patterns of organization of culture, usually also somewhat more complex than those which surround or precede them. However, since form and content are no more rigidly separable in culture than in living organisms, but rather constitute aspects of one another, a more highly patterned or richer organization tends strongly to be accompanied also by a greater accumulation of culture content or substance—by a larger number of countable items, spread over a wider range of human activities and expressed through more sharply differentiated activities.

Each culture segregation begins on a small scale, and many such beginnings must die again, overtaken and crowded out by others, which also mostly are submerged in their turn. Now and then, however, through the favor of some accident of history or nature, the little societies of a region forge or spurt ahead of their neighbors, reshaping their culture to a more effective adaptation, a greater assimilativeness, a more consistent selectiveness. Once such an advantage is gained, it is likely to be retained for a time, and in some cases it will be enhanced. The process thus tends to be self-perpetuatingly cumulative, but for a correspondingly smaller number of cultures whose area and population increase.

It is in series of events such as these that we must see—and in a measure we already do see, through archaeology—the localized beginnings of higher civilization in China and India, in Mesopotamia and Egypt; and again in Mexico and Peru. But for each of these cases of cultural growth continued to the attainment of farming, metal arts, larger populational units, political organization into states, urbanization, writing, and the other hallmarks of "civilization," there must have been several other nearly parallel beginnings that slowed and withered, or met disaster, or were absorbed. It is as part of this sort of natural order of events that the births of civilizations have to be regarded: as the few most successful and enduring concatenations of patterned culture out of many more that also began but did not culminate: —and not as rare miracles without precedent. Precedents or parallels must always exist—indeed, they prove to be there, on small or medium scale, as soon as we are willing to look for them among the data of history.

What follows is a survey of some of the more conspicuous formations in the direction of incipient but only partly achieved higher civilization among the non-literate natives of North America.

Native North America

At about the Panuco and the Lerma or Grande de Sur rivers, the pre-Columbian high culture of Guatemala and southern Mexico ended. To the north, there were still towns and principalities, in some areas; but nothing any longer that could be called cities, or attempts at tribute empires, or even vestiges of writing or artificially contrived calendars. In some areas, especially the large arid interior drainage basin north of the Valley of Mexico, the cultural decline was geographically sudden and steep; gatherers and hunters almost abutted on nationalities that were still within the high civilization. Aboriginal northern Mexico as a whole is very imperfectly known. The Spanish explorers and conquerors found only an anticlimax to what they had just subjugated in the south, reported it meagerly, and proceeded to wipe out the native culture, in most parts, even more effectively than they had higher cultures. Archaeological pickings are much slimmer than in the high-culture area. Therefore very much less has been done: enough to show that there are unlikely to be any great ruins or lost cities in northern Mexico, but not enough to allow us to define with much assurance any groups or tracts of markedly superior or highly distinctive development.

In Anglo-America, on the contrary, the native cultures, except on the Atlantic coast, mostly lasted, with some modifications but as still basically aboriginal fabrics, into the nineteenth century. In spots, they remained essentially intact until the middle of that century; and in many parts full memory pictures of native culture were obtainable from the old people who had been brought up in it, until the earlier decades of the present century. The United States and Canada were thus a bountiful area for ethnographers, and basic information on the historic native cultures is now available with an unusual degree of continuous coverage. Prehistory has also had a remarkable development in the past thirty years, ever since, after an initial wavering hesitation, North American archaeologists became aware that problems of cultural succession in time were soluble.

Three regions held cultures that stood out above the rest in elaborateness, definition, and systematization. One of these was the Southwestern United States, especially as represented by the town-dwelling Pueblo Indians. A second was the Southeast, from the lower Mississippi to Georgia. This area was less sharply characterized and less clearly delimited than the Southwestern culture. Proliferations of it extended at one time or another into Oklahoma and Nebraska, into Wisconsin, at an early period into Ohio, and later into central New York. The third region of distinctive native cultures was the Northwest Coast, namely the Pacific ocean frontage and coastal rivers[2] between Cape Mendocino in northern California and Yakutat in southern Alaska. This last was a wholly non-planting and non-breeding culture—perhaps the most elaborate such culture in the world.

In addition it will be necessary to make some reference to the historically late culture of the Indians of the Great Plains, which has so

2. Up the Columbia to the Dalles, the Fraser to about Harrison Lake, up the other streams more or less to their heads.

impressed the popular imagination of Americans as to develop into a stereotype into which all variant concepts of Indians and their life tended to be pressed. There are also the Eskimo, whom Toynbee has elevated into one of his two dozen civilizations, albeit an "arrested" one.

"Pueblos" meant simply "towns" to the Spaniard, but through usage as an adjective qualifying "Indians," the word has in English come to be the generic proper name applied to the town-dwelling peoples of New Mexico and Arizona, in distinction from those living in scattered hamlets or in villages of brush huts there or elsewhere. For the last twelve hundred years the Pueblos have built their houses of stone masonry; for the past thousand years they have clustered them compactly, room to room, and have lived a genuine town life. They did not work metals, but they wove cotton cloth, made high-grade pottery, and in general showed reasonable proficiency in a variety of technologies—more perhaps than any other group of Indians in the United States. The most powerful trend in their culture is the one toward ritualism. Prayers, songs, myths, dances, accoutrements, sacred fetishes, altars, symbolic paintings, membership and degrees in religious societies, a long array of both public and esoteric ceremonies—all these are strictly, elaborately, and repetitively formalized and put into set order and interrelation. Uniquely among North American Indians, the Pueblos have suppressed in their society the shaman—who receives personalized supernatural power from dreams, vision trances, or spirit possession—by converting him into a priest, or an official of a standardized curing society, who follows an ordained and established ritual instead of his individualized inner impulses. Similarly, the emotional shock of life crises—birth, adolescence, death—is softened by the Pueblos: taboos among the Pueblos are light and few, overt fear is toned down. If we add that violence is infrequent among the Pueblos, and that war was looked upon as an evil rather than a glory, and that alcoholic indulgence, which has ritual association and sanction all through Mexico to the borders of Pueblo territory, has never been accepted by them, it is evident why Zuni, and by implication Pueblo culture in general, has been characterized as Apollonian, unfrenetic, classical in its set or ethos. One may consider any such single epithet inadequate for the psychological characterization of a culture. But that the orientation of the culture is as just sketched. is admitted by all who know it through experience. The formalizing ritual tendencies were perhaps developed and associated as a mechanism for attaining the "Apollinian" calm and serenity sought; and the Pueblo definiteness in placement, technology, style, manners seems to be in its turn a facet of their formalism.

Pueblo distinctiveness is sharpened on comparison with their non-Pueblo neighbors. A branch of the Apache, migrants into the Southwest at some unknown time, probably not too far antedating the Spaniards, and now known as Navaho, proved adaptive to certain aspects of Spanish and American economy such as sheep raising, have multiplied, and have by now territorially almost engulfed Pueblo groups like the Zuni and Hopi. They have also taken over much native culture from the Pueblos: corn planting, cloth weaving, a great many ritual elements.

Altar paintings with dry earths and minerals, for instance, are made by the Navaho more elaborately and frequently than by the Pueblos from whom they learned them. Yet they are painted not in a fixed ceremony performed for the general good by the members of a permanent society, but by an individual who has learned his rite privately from another individual and performs it for the better health of another individual whose family engage him for the performance. There are possibly as many different Navaho "chants" and "ways" as Pueblo dances and ceremonies, but they are not organized into a balanced system, executed by recognized priests, nor ordered into a calendar. They remain just an aggregation of more or less varying but individually separate curing rites. Most of what is fixed at Hopi or Zuni—the membership that performs a dance, the kiva in which they practice and dress, the particular plazas in which they appear in a certain order, the particular supernaturals impersonated in each ceremony—all this has almost no Navaho counterpart. Each singer or curer there knows his own chant or chants, performs them with little reference to others and their rites, and when and where it is convenient. It is the difference between a highly and definitely organized culture —perhaps an over-organized one—and another perhaps nearly equally varied and rich in content, but much more loosely institutionalized, personalized in expression, and *ad lib* in execution.

Note: Go on to Apache and Walapai

I think it will be evident why the Pueblos are regarded by American ethnographers as constituting the focus or climax of Southwestern culture. Also how another culture can be so much more meager, less defined, shiftless, ineffective than Pueblo and yet have its content as truly "Southwestern" in character.

So far we have viewed the living culture of the recent Pueblos and their neighbors. Now to see it in depth as revealed by prehistory.

Archaeologically the arid Pueblo country has good preservation conditions, its open cover is easily explored; it is rich in ruins, and very rich in a varied pottery that serves as the readiest clue to unravel the details and intricacies of relationships and sequence. The Pueblo area was the first in Anglo-America to have its main successions of culture correctly recognized and solidly established. Then came the technique of absolute dating from tree-ring series—first developed in the same area. This finally carried the story back into the first century after Christ. Now radiocarbon dating of cave finds on the Tularasa has rolled Southwestern maize-planting—the ultimate foundation on which its sedentary culture rests—back to the third century B.C. In another cave, maize is thought to have begun to be deposited more than 2000 years earlier still—though this has not been incontrovertibly confirmed by radiocarbon tests. At any rate, it will be evident that the history of Southwestern culture is unusually full and exact for one that flourished wholly without writing.

It was recognized or assumed from the beginning of exploration that the ruins of the country were built by ancestors of the surviving Pueblos; then, that the picturesque cliff dwellings represented not a separate people but a transient local phase of Pueblo development. Next there were discovered the simple remains of an earlier culture, first thought to be the product of a non-Pueblo population, now believed to be at least mainly ancestral, who came to be called Basket Makers (on analogy with Cliff Dwellers and Mound Builders). Then a term Anasazi was coined, derived from a Navaho base, for the joint Basket Maker-Pueblo development. Eight uninterrupted Anasazi stages were recognized, three Basket Maker and five Pueblo, the last beginning with the Spanish suppression of the great Pueblo rebellion in 1692. On dendrochronological evidence, the transition from Basket Maker 3 to Pueblo 1, with the beginnings of stone masonry, falls around 700 A.D. Basket Maker 1 is a hypothetical stage, that is, undiscovered. It was reserved for a suspected pre-farming stage; for the Basket Maker 2 people already grew corn, though they began potteryless and have left remains that evidence their groping efforts to achieve the ceramic art.

The latter half of the Anasazi story is so fully documented by physically preserved remains that it will probably stand without serious modifications. The question remains whether the Anasazi culture did build up to a culmination and then enter upon a slow decline, as would be inferable from the name "Classical" often applied to Pueblo period 3, about 1050–1300 A.D.

I do not believe that this period contained the culmination of the entire Anasazi growth. What did climax then were certain features which the earlier explorations had impressed on us as typical of the pre-Spanish Pueblos: black-on-white geometrically decorated pottery, corrugated ware for cook pots, masonry rooms clustered into compact masses of several storeys, the semisubterranean circular kiva for ceremonial use.

With period Pueblo 4, polychrome ware increased in frequency and a glaze decoration appeared. Between them, they soon crowded out the black-on-white and corrugated styles. There were territorial shifts—abandonment of some tracts in the Southwest, appropriation of others. It was a time of change and transition. Towns were less impressively crowded than before, but as large if not larger. It is probable that when the Spaniards came, some two hundred years after the inception of period 4, they found a Pueblo culture richer in total inventory of content than in period 3, and patterned as definitely as then.

In period 4, accordingly, Pueblo culture was still developing beyond period 3. But it too was not "classical" in the sense of fifth-fourth century Greece, or Augustan Rome—namely, in being a climax. It is rather like the tumultuous European fifteenth to sixteenth centuries and the Italian Renaissance after the twelfth and thirteenth century tight ideational world of Aquinas and Dante, of supreme Catholic Christianity and Gothic arts. The old patterns were indeed relaxed, but relaxed in the process of enlarging their scope.

Coronado's horde of adventurers overran and conquered the Pueblos in 1540, but finding no ready riches, flowed out again, leaving behind the memory of a shock. Perhaps their chief impress on the Pueblos was the consciousness of outside forces stronger than they, against which, if they should irrupt again, their only defense would be unremitting passive resistance. The Spaniards did reappear before the century was out, and this time to stay, imposing their authority and their religion. The latter load must have galled the Pueblos particularly, seeing they had worked out with addiction their own elaborate ritual system. Tacit compromises of overt and covert coexistence of the two religions resulted, with Catholicism increasingly dominant along the Rio Grande, where the Spanish population was concentrated, but reduced to a thin veneer in the west among the remote Hopi. The New Mexican Spaniards were too far from their bases in Mexico, too few, and mostly too peasant-minded, to enslave the Pueblos as serfs, as their compatriots had done where it was profitable in Mexico. And they brought in a good many new conveniences by which the Pueblos profited and their culture was enriched: donkeys for loads, mutton to eat, wool to weave, peach trees and melons and onions, chimneys, windows, and adobe bricks, intertown peace. But the Indians were like Chinese in their pride in their culture, and were galled for all their imposed prosperity, and ate it in, and finally rose in the great rebellion of 1680 which swept every Spaniard and Mexican out of the country.

The Spanish came back once more and for good—here begins our Pueblo 5 period—and there was nothing left for the Indians but to submit and try to preserve tenaciously as much as they could of their own. It is significant that they did not to any serious degree, like so many unlettered peoples pressed upon by the civilized, pour all their aspirations into one last despair-born surge of illusion—a Messianic movement. Their rebellion was realistically conceived, and when it crashed this was realistically accepted. Period 5 was indeed a period of colonial decline for the Pueblos. It stifled them the more because the outer Spanish periphery of New Mexico and Santa Fe in many ways lagged a century behind Mexico and Lima, and therefore failed to participate in the eighteenth century revival of population and amelioration of social and economic conditions in Spanish America.

The following Mexican and American regimes were at least anti-clerical, and where enough of the old native ritual had remained intact as a system, Pueblo culture reconstituted itself about that system. Nor does it follow that this reorganized native culture of today will necessarily wither under the impact of tractors and schooling and wages. Americans have always had considerable sectarian tolerance, and their public toleration of the exotic and non-conformist is growing. If Hopi and Zuni religion can maintain its hold on its adherents—a hold which is probably stronger than the real activation of most Americans by Christianity—and can at the same time work out an adaptation to a reasonably successful economic standard, there is no reason why enough of native culture should not continue to function sufficiently to carry it into a Pueblo 6 period. The Navaho have indeed begun to do something of the sort; and while they are individually more ready to adapt, their culture lacks the definite, hard, tough coordination of Pueblo culture.

The number of people participating in a culture is always of some significance. There are today [19,329 (1950 Census)] Pueblo Indians, in about thirty towns, after several recent fissions. Earlier in this century, the population numbered under 10,000, the towns about twenty-five. Coronado in 1540 found around seventy towns. The population then is estimated at 34,000 by Mooney, at about 20,000 by Kidder. It certainly never exceeded, and probably never reached 50,000. This smallness of numbers reflected the historic fact that the Pueblos with all their distinctiveness did not achieve a great civilization.

I hesitate to speak here in terms of cause and effect, for while great civilizations seem to require fairly large populations, they also have the faculty or potentiality of drawing large populations within their range, or spreading themselves over them. There have been cultures of true originality and genuine distinctiveness carried by even fewer people than the Pueblo culture; but they have remained minor cultures.

However fine their patterning, it lacks breadth, and especially heft or mass, such as can apparently be achieved only by larger aggregations of social units.

Cultural nucleations rarely come singly. If the external preconditions and the internal impulses are favorable, we should expect them to bud into parallel or related starts several times in an area or era. This is true of the native Southwest. The most important sibling of the Anasazi culture was the Hohokam. This name denotes "the ancients" in the language of the Pima and Papago, who now live in the old Hohokam area of the Gila drainage in southern Arizona. The Hohokam were the southern neighbors and contemporaries of the Anasazi—somewhat more exactly, neighbors on the southwest. To the north of the Anasazi, especially in Utah, there are found some remains of reduced or "peripheral Pueblo" cultures, containing only part of the full Pueblo inventory, and the remainder nothing definite enough to warrant a larger name. But the Hohokam culture paralleled the Anasazi at point after point—sometimes alike, sometimes different, but normally equivalent. Instead of stone masonry, the Hohokam built dwellings of posts and reeds or wattle-and-daub; occasional mounmental structures were of rammed earth—what is called tapia in Latin America. Their habitat being the more arid, they irrigated from canals and ditches as the Anasazi did at best only intermittently and half-heartedly, and mostly not at all. They cremated their dead with offerings to them, instead of burying them. In place of black-on-white or corrugated, their ware was red-on-buff, and was smoothed with a paddle and anvil instead of a scraper. And so at dozens of other points. But they were like the Anasazi in being sedentary farmers in fair-sized settlements.

Living south of the Anasazi they should have been more exposed to Mexican influences, especially those influences penetrating up the Sinaloa-Sonora Pacific-side corridor of Mexico. Their archaeology manifests several South Mexican traits: mirrors of pyrites, ball courts, in one instance a ball of rubber, copper bells of Mexican origin, although their scattering use of these last was shared with the Anasazi. Something of this sort would be expectable from the respective positions.

Hohokam prehistory is dated by cross-ties of Anasazi objects, the timbers in their habitat not lending themselves to adequate dendrochronological technique. Roughly, the courses of the two cultures ran coeval. Five Hohokam periods have been set up, of which three are archaeologically recognized. I avoid the names—like Colonial, Sedentary, Classical—because they carry misleading implications. During Hohokam 3, influences from the Gila penetrated north into the western Anasazi periphery up to the San Francisco mountain massif, carrying with them even an occasional ball court (Sinagua culture). In Hohokam 4, Pueblo 3, a migratory Pueblo population penetrated south into Gila drainage, and became locally associated with Hohokam societies and accepted some degree of Hohokam culture. Incidentally, Salado was the first aspect to be described in the Hohokam area by archaeologists. Before the time the Salado culture ended around 1450, the Hohokam culture as a whole had disappeared. The Spaniards noted only its Casa Grande ruin, which is believed due to Salado Anasazi influence. Hohokam 5 refers to the historic Pima and Papago, as being either the changed descendants or the alien successors of the Hohokam. This final period is therefore speculative, that is, undocumented by archaeology, like the first Hohokam and first Anasazi periods. If the Hohokam 4 culture was replaced by Pima and Papago culture, particularly if it turned into it, the fact that these two tribes today possess rather close linguistic relatives as far south in Mexico as Durango and Jalisco is almost certain to have relevance to Hohokam history, either at its beginning or its end.

The fact that Hohokam culture melted away before Caucasians were in the land, whereas Anasazi maintains itself in some measure still, argues that the less tough and viable Hohokam was built on a slenderer base of content and that it failed to develop any one of its pattern systems to as trenchant a definition as, for instance, Anasazi ritual religiosity.

A third sprout of ancient sedentary pottery-making culture has been proposed for the Southwest: Mogollon in southwestern New Mexico, in the region of the upper Gila and the Mimbres. The facts are agreed on, their interpretation is controversial, some claiming for Mogollon equal taxonomic rank with Anasazi and Hohokam, others making it a variant or modification or early blend of them. The positive criteria of Mogollon culture are rather few, the most marked being a distinctive pottery tradition of brownware. This goes back pretty far in time, but the Mogollon shoot was not very vigorous and died out by the end of Pueblo 3, with the Mimbres culture. This Mimbres phase produced possibly the most distinctive and aesthetically original pottery art of the Southwest; but it was rather eclectically makeshift and indistinctive in its house types and other features. At that, it seems to be agreed that there went into the Mimbres ceramic style not only a Mogollon ingredient but a definite black-on-white Anasazi tradition; and what finally happened to the Mimbreños and upper Gileños is also not clear. In short, if Mogollon was a genuinely autonomous segregation of culture, we have three such root-related and neighboring parallel growths in the ancient Southwest; otherwise only two. The interplay and relation of these Southwestern cultures is comparable, on a small scale, to that between Maya and Aztec in Mexico in 1500 A.D., with Olmec and Toltec and Zapotec already declined then, and Mixtec and Tarascan still coming up, but all of them representing shoots from the same basic root-stock of civilization.

Characterize briefly Luiseño, Mohave, Yuma.

APPENDIXES

PRESENCES AND ABSENCES: OLD AND NEW WORLD CIVILIZATIONS

Many years ago Boas observed that with all the growth of elaborate civilization in parts of aboriginal America—the stretch from Mexico to Peru-Bolivia, sometimes called "nuclear native America"—there was lacking in all pre-Columbian New World societies a series of culture traits that had a wide and ancient distribution in Asia, Europe, and Africa. Such were the manufacture of iron, use of the wheel, the plow, stringed musical instruments, and the customs of riddles and proverbs. The first three at least are of such practical utility that it is hardly conceivable that they would ever have been given up once they were established among any society. Stringed instruments, riddles, and proverbs are of lesser importance, but they are basically simple devices which, speculatively, one might expect to have been invented or adopted in any reasonably rich civilization. They certainly occur in abundant development in many Old World cultures much simpler than those of the Aztec, Maya, and Inca that lacked them.

From this not previusly recognized set of negative distributions Boas drew two inferences, one theoretical, the other historical.

The theoretical conclusion was that extreme caution is called for in regard to believing that specific inventions or institutions flow automatically or spontaneously out of "human nature," that is, out of the inherent constitution of the human mind, as culture reaches certain stages or degrees of elaboration. Basically, this critical principle remains valid today.[1]

1. True, a highly industrialized technology wholly lacking knowledge of the principle of the wheel is hardly conceivable. But this means merely that the wheel is a presumably necessary *precondition* of civilization attaining a rich and advanced technology.

The historical inference is that the higher native American cultures could not well have been derived outright or even mainly from those of the Old World, else they would have retained the extraordinarily useful knowledge of wheel, plow, and iron extraction. By and large, they must have undergone the bulk of their development independently on American soil. Pre-Columbian cultural transfers between the two hemispheres are not denied, but must in each case be specifically proved instead of assumed, and are probably responsible for only a minority fraction of the total cultural inventory of the native New World. Overwhelmingly, this view continues to be held by American ethnographers and archaeologists.

I wish now to add to the Boas list a further series of inventions and institutions apparently wholly lacking in the native New World although possessing ancient and wide distribution in the Old. These are:

Philosophy
Alchemy
Alphabetic writing
Coins
Monasticism
Castration and eunuchism
Games of purely mental skill
Blood sacrifice
Systems of divination from organs of the body (hepatoscopy)
Oaths, curses, and blessings
The scapegoat
Trial by ordeal

Obviously such a list is significant only for items that are pretty rigorously definable. Absences must be total from America if they are to mean something, and the things that are absent must be separably identifiable. If cultural items shade into one another, they lose force in the present connection. Coins and alphabets possess such definiteness for what they include and exclude; valuables and writing do not. These latter do occur in the New as well as the Old World, and the specific constitution and content—usually called "form" by writers on culture—of their several occurrences can be quite diverse. Coins and alphabets however contain a uniform, constant core of particular features by definition. The defining features for the traits listed will be set forth or adumbrated below.

What is also important is that all known coinages seem derived from an invention made in Western Asia Minor in the seventh century B.C. All alphabets are derived from an invention made in the vicinity of Palestine around 1500 B.C. "Derived" here means literal transfer of knowledge from one society to another, a historic derivation, a learning or reapplication of something learned. Coinage and the alphabetic manner of writing thus are unitary historic entities, however much their forms ramify and diverge externally in their spread through time and space. This unity is long since a commonplace of historic knowledge for coins and alphabets, but will need substantiation below, and perhaps qualification, for some of the other items in the list.

As contrasted with absences in the New World, the Old has since a long time conspicuously shared much of its basic civilization over a large part of its greater area—from western Europe to Japan and the East Indies, along with Africa north of the Sahara and sometimes south of it. The same basic food plants, especially barley, wheat, and millet, have been in cultivation in this area since agriculture was devised. The most important domesticated animals have been kept—cattle, sheep, goats, swine, later the ass and the horse. The plow was early in use, then the wheel for transport and for milling, then the stirruped saddle. Iron working was added to copper and bronze casting in western Asia, then in eastern and in Europe and in Africa. Probably the largest number of these fundamental increments to civilization were developed in the region of southwestern Asia, and spread out from there northwest into Europe, westward into Egypt and Africa, and east as far as the limit of Chinese and Indian cultural influence. But other elements were first controlled or devised in the Far East—rice and chickens and perhaps the pig, porcelain and silk—and their extension was westward. Only the peripheral regions remained without most of this cultural inventory—Australia, the outer Pacific islands, the Siberian tundra, to some extent south Africa. Wherever culture was not too backward in the Old World through remoteness or adversely limiting environment, it tended to be based on the same fundamental stock of acquisitions and inventions; to which then each region or nation added its characteristic specializations, or a particular cast in which it reexpressed them.

Some decades ago the geographer Ratzel revived the old Greek term Oikoumenê—originally denoting the inhabited world—with the meaning of this core and larger part of the eastern hemisphere that shared the fundamentals just enumerated and that contained also all the several greater civilizations developed in ancient and modern times. He even mapped the Oikoumenê as he mapped the extension of the plow. A few years ago, I revived the term and concept, with emphasis on how much the societies comprised within its range shared beyond basic subsistence and technology. I instanced eunuchism, blood sacrifice, liver divination, the composite and later the cross bow, gunpowder, felt, money, water mills, falconry, the compass, the game of chess, the alphabet, printing, grammar, the week, monasticism, astrology, alchemy, and philosophy. Not all of these became established quite everywhere in the Oikoumenê. Western Europe resisted eunuchism, China the institutions of the week and the zodiac. China, India, and Islam all took over the system of lunar stations or mansions, Christian Europe did not.

But these non-participations were exceptional. Mostly, some knowledge of new institutions or inventions became spread over the whole tricontinental mass, even backward societies often accepting fragments or adaptations of them.

Now it is obvious that the inventory just cited as characterizing the Oikoumenê is also very nearly the list enumerated as lacking from even the highest civilizations of native America, or would become such if cultural items that have been omitted from the native American list because of their mere obviousness or lateness—such as gunpowder, falconry, compass, water mills—were included in it.

The same two principles inferred from the absences in the native New World therefore appear to be corroborated by the presences of the same features in the Old World Oikoumenê: namely, first, that the enumerated important components of culture are not spontaneous or automatic or necessary in the growth of civilization, but, second, that they each represent specific historic developments; particularistic, not immanent, and therefore in a sense accidental.

With these two major inferences at stake, I shall now briefly consider how far the suggested absences from native America can actually be validated as a significant counterpart of their wide occurrence in the Oikoumenê.

Since full citation of negative evidence tends to be endless, consideration will be centered on definition of features. In regard to a conceptually delimited cultural device or institution Americanist opinion can be readily mobilized and voiced, as regards presence and absence. It will thus be available for the test of contrast or likeness with the Old World.

SCIENCE

The history of science in the Old World is proving more complex as we learn more about it. For instance, what Greek astronomy derived from Neo-Babylonian is now seen as a much larger component than it was fifty years ago. The sources of Indian and Chinese mathematics and astronomy are still exceedingly obscure, as are what they may have contributed to the West. I shall refrain altogether from entering on this vast subject, and confine myself here to a reappraisal of what native Americans did and did not achieve in science.

They have to their credit some definite and spectacular attainments, especially the long-count calendar of the Maya, the determination of planetary revolution periods, and their devising a symbol for zero. But there is some reason for believing that these accomplishments were slender pinnacles springing from a narrow base. The range of Maya and other American science, in theory, in mass of knowledge, and in technological application proves surprisingly limited.

[*Ed. note: The following list of topics relates to the nature of native American scientific achievement.*]

positive 0
over-all totals give accur. obs. + counting

no theory known
no geometry
no △ sq
arithm. of nos.

no fract. or recipr.
no physics

Divination, etc.

Entrail divination *vs.* *various divination*
Scapulomancy
[dom. anim. ?? Chin. tort]
Jap. deer]
Oath *vs.* *Affirmation, Vituperation*
Curse, Blessing
Puns (folk-etymology—Dakota)
Life Ordeal *vs.* *Divination*
poison, fire, water *or Tests*
Combat Ordeal

Scapegoat
Eunuchism

Alchemy
(Astrology)
Philosophy

Games of Mental skill
Cubical dice

Bowed stringed instrum.

Monasticism *Candles, lamps, tonsure*

Possession (by god
(causes illness
non-Amer.
Coined money
Printing, seals—for identif or multipl
(cloth)

Grammar
Verse meter

Cross-bow
Falconry
Felt

1. Liver or entrail divination, probably a by-product of altar sacrifice of domestic animals, is evidently a single growth and diffusion over the full breadth of the Eurasian Oikoumenê to Borneo and Luzon. It is most familiar to us from the Greeks and Romans; the earliest known instance is the cuneiform inscribed pottery model of a liver from [Babylonia (2100 B.C.)].

There seems to have been no native American systematic divination from the entrails of animals. This absence would be expectable if American life or blood sacrifice represented an historic growth separate from the Old World one. Such a separateness may be suspected and is in need of analysis. For one thing, while animal sacrifice extends as far as the Chukchi, it stops abruptly with Bering Strait. The Iroquois White Dog sacrifice seems to be post-Columbian. The Pueblos kept not only dogs but turkeys, yet sacrificed neither. A few California cases relate to captured animals like occasional eagles and bears, and their context seems very different. In high-culture Mexico, and from there south to Andean Peru-Bolivia, life sacrifice is preeminently human sacrifice. The emphasis is on tearing out the heart or on decapitation, both uncharacteristic of the Old World. There is if anything more emphasis on blood; but little if any burnt offering. In Mexico the human victim was dressed in the insignia of the god, and often he was flayed and his fresh skin was put on and danced in by a priest: the god Xipe even is *"the flayed one." Frazer, with his free-association method of viewing all ramifications of magic as integrally connected—as they are on the psychological level of potential human nature—connects these specific Mexican emphases with divine king killing, dying god, and fertility rejuvenation concepts and practices of the Old World. Culturally and historically, however, the focus of modern interpretation is on differential characterization as the basis of meaningful synthesis; and Mexican human sacrifice seems more distinctive than it seems like Old World sacrifice in its elements and its weighting.*

Animal sacrifice certainly was infinitely less developed in Mexico than in the Old World. The most important victims were quails! It is true that domestic animals were of far less consequence in America, and the failure to develop plow and wheel may be in part a function of the fact. Yet the Mexicans had dogs, turkeys, and Muscovy ducks, and raised the former for food. In the Andes, llama and alpaca were available, and were sacrificed; apparently dogs and guinea-pigs were not.

. . . .

All in all it may be fair to say that there is no clear evidence of pre-Columbian entrail divination in America, and that while there was sacrifice it was so differently weighted in its constituents and patterns that it is unlikely to be connected with Old World sacrifice by more than stimulus diffusion.

1b. In contrast with entrail divination, Cooper has shown that shoulder-blade divination did cross Bering Strait into America. The earliest known prototype of this is in Shang China: a heated point pressed against tortoise shell. The westward spread, most of it much later, generally used sheep shoulder blades; though by the time the practice reached Europe and Africa, the application of heat had generally been given up. The eastward spread also concentrated on shoulder blades, but prevailingly of wild animals: in ancient Japan, of the stag; Koryak, seal; Chukchi, domestic reindeer; American subarctic forest, caribou and moose—still scorched. The Eskimo, the Northwest Coast Indians, all those south of the coniferous belt, did not adopt the custom.

This shoulder blade-scorching item shows that the Oikoumenê finds no inviolable limit at the Pacific Ocean. With typological and areal distribution even half as clean-cut for entrail divination, we would have to concede the probability that it had been carried from Asia to America.

2. Fully developed oaths, curses, and blessings are at least dubious in native America. Definition is the first requisite in this case. Old Testament examples will serve:

Abr. thigh
Covenant Noah
Exodus
Deborah

Jericho
Jacob, Isaac, Moses
The common element in these is a certain formalism.

PHILOSOPHY

By philosophy I understand, in cultural-historical context, something more than the occasional reflections of peasants, Eskimos, or any essentially illiterate peoples, shrewd and profound as these sometimes are. I would define philosophy as coordinated abstract thinking on the nature of the universe, of being, of ourselves as men, and of our knowing; with the employment of words in a consistent manner until some of them become essentially precise or "technical" terms, usable in the erection of a systematic conceptual structure, which in turn is capable of enlargement or serving as foundation for further systematizing. While there may be in philosophy an emotional suffusion leading to mysticism, there may not be emotional dominance, for with prevalence of connotation over denotation terminological rigor is lost, and therewith rational concatenation into conceptual system. There must of course be essential freedom from magic and ritual. A final criterion is recognition as philosophy by subsequent or alien philosophies.

Philosophy, thus circumscribed, originated in human culture simultaneously around 600–500 B.C. among Chinese, Indians, Iranians, and Greeks. The simultaneity is as striking as it is unexplained, especially since all subsequent philosophies are partly derivative from these first four. I have shown elsewhere that mathematical probability would allow such simultaneity to occur as a random coincidence once in the known history of culture. This of course means that untraced causal relations between the four simultaneities need not be invoked; it does not mean that causal relations have been disproved. However, no satisfactory indication of connections or common dependence on an underlying factor has yet been adduced.

I would admit philosophizings, but deny systematic philosophy as here defined, to the ancient Near Eastern nations—Sumerians, Babylonians, Hebrews, and Egyptians.

It is also clear that no American people had achieved a systematic philosophy.

Because philosophy uses language as its tool; because it is always preceded by that universal, religion, which also often gives quasi-answers to some of the same questions; and because languages and religions long grew up specifically quite diverse according to their region: therefore philosophy is a cultural activity whose principal manifestations are on their face independent. Therewith they are in a different class from for instance the week or the alphabet, whose variant forms have been without very much difficulty historically traceable as all derived from a single origin. If the question is here raised whether the independence of philosophies is total, or whether common stimuli were shared by them, it is because many sharply defined advanced cultural products prove on assemblage and analysis of the facts to be, like the week and the alphabet, historic diversifications from single origins. There are so many of them, indeed, that some suspicion is in order about those activities, like philosophy, that still seem independent and multiple in origin.

Now, while the discovery that the hundreds of seemingly so different alphabets all stem from one source, was not too arduous, it did require detailed, careful, point-for-point, comparison. However, correspondingly specific positive evidence of historic derivation between the several early philosophies has as yet not been brought forward, though they are fairly well known. I have only two suggestions to offer that may bear on the question. These suggestions are, first, the inverse relation—historic and perhaps functional also—between philosophy and religion and pseudo-science; and second, the relation between philosophy and poetry. These points will be discussed below, under the topics of alchemy-astrology, and poetry.

POETRY

"Poetry" is here used in the narrow sense of speech employed for aesthetically emotional effect in some regularly recurring formal auditory pattern or structure that is analyzable and definable. The pattern may be qualitative, as in rhyme, assonance, or alliteration; or quantitative as regards words, syllables, stress accents, tone, or length of syllables; or combinations of these. This pattern applies to the basic definable or metric unit of pattern, the verse or line; verses again may be patterned, as into stanzas. There may also be subdivision of the unit or verse, as by a caesura; or permissible substitution as of spondee for dactyl in Latin and Greek, or so-called anapest for iamb in modern English and German. In full poetry, the extent of such alternatives is strictly determined. Any or all of these features give poetical speech the quality of being "metrical." That is, it is measured or bound or regulated in form, as compared with normal speech or "prose" which is relatively unstructured or freely varied in its patterns according to sense. Briefly, poetry achieves aesthetic effect by imposing a formal sound structure on the intrinsic sense or meaning.

This definition has been made as narrow as possible, with emphasis on form alone, in order that it may be precise. Obviously, certain emotional prose may be more "poetical" in its effect, more aesthetically stimulating or satisfying, than certain poetry wholly regular in form but banal in content or vapid in emotional charge. Aesthetic effects however are notoriously subjective and variable, and in culture-historical inquiries, as distinct from aesthetic appraisal, form, which is largely definable objectively, is the successful operational criterion.

At that, there remain some intergradations, such as rhyming prose in oratorical Arabic. Shakespearean blank verse can be stressed down in recital to simulate prose; but its basic regularity of structure quickly becomes evident on analysis, as it would sooner or later become evident to the ear unless disguised by deliberate contortions. On the other hand, in Walt Whitman's typical "verse," though it is written in lines and generally accepted as poetry, irregularity of formal structure prevails. Its claim to being poetry rests upon the historical fact that it is a derivative or end-product of verse, a decomposition of poetry which, through a development of style, has largely made the return to prose. There is "rhythm," but it is mostly "free" or variable in pattern. The so-called poetry of the ancient Near East has perhaps even less claim than Whitman to be counted as such, because it precedes measurable form without attaining it.

Actual songs with words require discrimination. It is a question of which element determines. We generally "set" poems to music; a ballad or Chou shih may repeat a melody for progressive stanzas. But many primitives fit words to a melody, with indefinite distortion to meet the rhythm of the music, or with free filling by meaningless expletives; whereas, spoken naturally, the same words may totally lack metrical form. Such assemblages of words, whose form is wholly or preponderantly in their musical rendering, are not counted as poetry here. There are also cases—at least alleged ones—of poems and melodies being composed simultaneously. This seems successfully possible, as a general practice, only if either the verbal or the melodic form is simple and inclined to repetitiveness. At any rate such instances of complete fusion or aesthetic ambivalence may not be taken as characteristic of poetry in general. One can indeed hold a hypothesis that poetry "originated" from song—as some would find the origin of song in dance—but this is only speculation, unverifiable today.

If now we turn from definition to the historical array, there seems no evidence that any pre-Columbian American people ever achieved unsung metrical form of any regularity, free from European influence. The "Inca drama" Ollantay resolves into a composition by a monk who knew Quechua.

There is nothing astonishing in this absence when one recalls that formally marked poetry was equally lacking from the advanced civilizations of the ancient Near East: Sumerians, Babylonians and Assyrians, Egyptians, Hebrews. Among all these peoples, an equivalent of poetry can be distinguished from prose, in that it is cast as a balancing in expression: sometimes of contrast, more often of repetition of idea in new words. Also, there is more figurative expression than in narrative or normal prose. The Biblical Psalms and Proverbs are familiar examples; also Lamech's song and Deborah's, and the Blessings of Jacob and Moses. There is no doubt that these passages were felt as being about as distinct from ordinary speech as our verse is felt to be. And we too can recognize their qualitative separateness. The point is, we cannot define their form as something regular. The specifically poetic pattern of form cannot be abstracted from the content of meaning. Such form as there is is embodied in the sense or thought, not separable out by any fixed scheme or recurrent system of syllables, length, stresses, tones, or rhymes.

As a matter of fact, no mechanism even as pseudo-formal or quasi-regular as Biblical or Mesopotamian balance has yet been recognized in any native American literary product.

Egyptian, indeed, shows some tendency to alliteration and a kind of punning—an allusive use of similar sounding words. Neither technique is obligatory or developed at all systematically. They are, comparatively, of interest chiefly as incomplete attempts at what on the one hand—as regards alliteration—the early Germanic peoples much later made the chief criterion of their verse, and on the other—as regards double meaning—the Japanese carried much farther than the Hamites on the lower Nile.

Indubitable poetry appears only around 1000 B.C. in three places outside the Near East: Greece, China, and India, in three separate forms which evidently originated independently of one another.

The earliest known Greek meter was the epic hexameter, based on a pattern of long and short syllables, variable in alternative detail—dactyls and spondees—within a rigorously fixed pattern.

Chinese Chou and perhaps Shang dynasty meters counted syllables —four or sometimes five to a line—grouped these into stanzas, and used end-rhyme. The known examples are lyric and were also sung.

Indian poetry can in part be traced back to an earlier date than Greek or Chinese if we count in the hymns of the Rig Veda. These already have meters of a fixed number of syllables, the last three to five of which are arranged in a definite pattern of vowel lengths. Subsequent classical Sanskrit literature extended the quantitative pattern to cover the whole line, and after about 1000 A.D. rhyme was superadded in the poet-classical vernaculars.

The story of subsequent developments of poetical form the world over is a long and complicated one, whose totality has never been brought together in a comparison interested both in divergent originalities and in repetitive parallels. One need only instance the forms of the Edda and the Kalevala, early Latin Saturnian meter, the rise of rhyme and assonance in Europe, of quantitatively patterned poetry in Arabic and Persian, of mere syllable-allotting to lines in Japanese.

Strange as it may seem, there was evidently an early connection between metrical poetry and systematic philosophy. China, India, and

Greece, which first developed verse, followed some centuries later—again independently—in being also the first to develop philosophy. This may be coincidence, but more likely is correlation. And it is remarkable. Established poetical form would make for a new kind of language consciousness, which presumably might be a potent aid when the first strivings for coherent abstract expression came to the fore. The segregation out of an awareness of form in speech, on this hypothesis, made possible a more effective concentration on consistent and precise denotation of words, as compared with the previous magma of indifferentiated [sic] speech. After all, we of today so take for granted poetry and literary expression, and again technical terminology for rigorous intellectual purposes—both distinct from everyday common speech—that it requires an effort to imagine ourselves still using only an indifferentiated language such as a Near Easterner of the second pre-Christian millennium alone had available.

In favor of the connection there is also the fact of occurrence of philosophy expressed in poetry in all three civilizations—least perhaps in China, longest in India, continuing in the Graeco-Roman world down to Lucretius; but not seriously subsequently. The reassociation would be a phase in the larger process of segregation.

THE TIME PROFILE OF WESTERN CIVILIZATION

OUR own civilization, the Western, grew up largely on the European part of the soil previously occupied by the Roman half of the Hellenic or Graeco-Roman or Classical civilization, but with some extensions beyond the former Roman frontier, as in Germany. The time of its beginning may be set somewhere between 500 and 900.

Toynbee says before 700. One might shade this more narrowly to 650, as the date perhaps marking most closely the nadir of barbarization intervening between the past Classical and the coming Western civilization. Spengler says 900, or sometimes tenth century, in referring to the birth of the Western culture; but with a gestation or "prodromal" period since 500.

In favor of the recognition of such an embryonic stage there are the following facts. By 500 all of the Roman west was in barbarian power and political control, and the old Classical culture was in clear disintegration there; but nothing was yet apparent that was qualitatively suggestive of the future European civilization. However, around 900 or soon after, as Spengler observes, the main modern nationalities of western Europe emerged: that is, they attained consciousness of themselves as nationalities. The first historical appearance of the French and German languages, as distinct from Latin and from Germanic vernaculars, is in a tenth-century record of the Strasbourg oaths which the grandsons of Charlemagne gave each other in 842. Spengler's prodromal phase of 500–900 has the merit of doing something, conceptually, with Charlemagne's empire and the so-called Carolingian cultural renaissance. This Carolingian renaissance obviously underlay all Western civilization chronologically; and yet it left so little impress on this civilization as to be puzzling. If it was a revival, how could it have so little permanent effect? Was it therefore perhaps an abortive endeavor rather than an actual revival? In fact, in the century after Charlemagne, everything Carolingian disintegrated[1]—the empire with its internationalism as well as much of the meager little rebirth of culture. By contrast, the basic alignments that emerged during the following tenth century—whether national, social, or cultural alignments—have persisted until today under all the enrichments and modifications that have been added to them.

It has always been a question of what the Carolingian empire and unification of western Christian Europe—and this was the only political unification that Europe ever attained!—what Charlemagne's empire really meant, on long-range view. Apparently its significance lay in its declaration of autonomy. Charles the Great's empire declared the westerly Graeco-Roman civilization definitely dead, and the West now independent of the Byzantine survival of easterly Graeco-Roman civilization. Hence the suddenly overt tensions between West and East within the Christian Church at this period.[2] But the West was still too poor in material wealth and in cultural content to develop a real civilization under Charlemagne. So it had to begin over again, and much less pretentiously, a century or more later, when the Carolingian empire had not only fallen to pieces but had been definitely superseded by the emerged nationalistic consciousness.

Western civilization has throughout remained multinational, "polyphonic and orchestral," as it then began in the 900's. It is of very real significance that Charlemagne's unification has never yet been successfully imitated in Europe, though Spaniards, French and Germans[3] successively have tried; and Russians are apparently now trying. Pre-

1. The weakness accompanying the Carolingian disintegration is pregnantly illustrated by the fact that the peak period of Viking raiding and spoliation of the continent fell between 830 and 900.

2. The tensions and rift are instanced by the Pope's crowning of Charlemagne as Caesar in 800; by Charlemagne's intervention in the *filioque* doctrinal dispute in 809; by the council of [Constantinople, 869–870] and the quarrel of Photius with the Popes [Nicholas I and Leo VI]; [and] by the contest of the eastern and western churches for the adhesion of Bulgaria.

3. Reference is to Hitler, not to the mediaeval Holy Roman Empire, which was always an unrealized dream nostalgic for a form. Even the Italians, whom in a sense this mediaeval pseudo-empire exalted, were for the most part opposed to it.

cedent is therefore against the Russians, if they belong to the Western civilization. Whereas if they represent an essentially separate civilization, as Danilevsky contended, there is no precedent for or against their prospects. In that case, the "youth" of Russian culture may mean either that it possesses greater vigor and strength than the older Western civilizations, or that it is characterized by greater immaturity and fumbling.

The basic multinationalism of Western civilization is also evident from the fact that it had hardly begun to crystallize out when, within a generation of the year 1000, there were added to the French and German consciousnesses a further series of emerging nationalities: Polish,[4] Hungarian, Scandinavian, English,[5] which have persisted.[6]

We may therefore conclude that at some time between 500 and 650 or 700 the essential detachment of western Europe from Graeco-Roman civilization became effective; that from 650–700 on this autonomy began to come into the consciousness of western societies and that these tended to assume first political cohesion and then national scope; and that around 900 or 950 the framework of the new culture began to fill, however humbly at first, with cultural content of its own creation. By 1100, with the Crusades, the youthful Western society had already become aggressive against the societies of the Byzantine and Arab Islamic civilizations—impracticably aggressive as regards permanent expansion, it is true, but nevertheless actually successful for a time.

This Western civilization is at the moment the dominant one in the world. Its ending has been repeatedly forecast: as follows. By Danilevsky, it was forecast to happen soon, whenever Russia shall become consolidated; because the West is already overripe. By Spengler, the prediction is for about 2200, Caesarism and the "civilization" phase having been entered on around 1800. By Toynbee, the end threatens

4. Russia also attained its first national organization around 1000, but is not included here because this early state still lay wholly outside the Roman Catholic and Western sphere of influence.

5. Decision would have to be made as between Canute the Dane, 1014–35, or Alfred [848–899], with the latter construed as preceding 1000 because of English geographical nearness to the Frankish-North French center.

6. There is a brief tabular collocation in my Configurations, p. 726.

and is indicated by numerous warning symptoms. This end may possibly happen soon, but it is by no means inevitable, because ultimate resources are moral and religious, and are therefore beyond real predictability. For my part, I refrain from long-range prophecy. It is tempting but usually unprofitable, practically as well as intellectually: its emotional repercussions tend to be high, its probability values low.

The course of this Western civilization of ours is remarkable for the strong degree of difference of content between its two main phases, which are usually called the Mediaeval and the Modern. The first, which culminated in the twelve hundreds and really ended soon after 1300, is characterized by the power and success of the Church. It was in the High Mediaevalism of the West that Christianity reached the crowning success of its career. Christianity at that time achieved an organization and domination of society that were not only extraordinarily effective but were culturally productive and concordant. Mediaeval philosophy, architecture, and art are thoroughly religious and at the same time embody secular values of a high order. Other branches of Christianity—Greek, Slavic, Nestorian—were equally sincere and fervid, but they failed to produce even rudiments of anything comparable either aesthetically or intellectually.

Around 1300 and the ensuing decades the tight High Mediaeval Christian frame began to be unable to contain any longer the cultural creativity that was swelling within it. The earlier satisfaction afforded by mere existence within this frame, the essential indifference or hostility to everything outside it, now commenced to disappear. Knowledge of what lay beyond, knowledge of the past, secular knowledge became more and more sought. Religious feeling weakened, at least relatively. The Church as an organization fell into troubles: there happened the attempt of Anagni, the Popes at Avignon, the Great Papal Schism, the Hussite Revolt, the Councils that failed to result in reforms. Systematic scholastic philosophy virtually died as knowledge increased by leaps and bounds—knowledge of the world as well as inventions and technologies: gunpowder, printing, oil painting, seaworthy ships, spectacles, clocks, playing cards, Arabic numerals and algebra, casting of iron and other metallurgical processes. Not one of these had anything to do with religion or furthered religion, but they all enriched the civilization and the life under it. The Gothic arts continued for a time, on momentum. But they showed definite symptoms of decadence: flamboyancy, perpendicularity; or they were applied secularly to guild halls and tomb monuments, not to cathedrals. The Mediaeval profane vernacular literatures, lyrical and narrative, now became arid, allegorizing, or extravagant. Even the political structure shook. The monarchies receded from such mild strength as they had attained in the thirteenth century. Towns grew in wealth and strength but also in embroilments; feudalism was losing its hold, but no substitute for it had forged into consciousness. Politically, the two centuries were centrifugal and disruptive; in Spain and Germany as in France and England royal power receded.

Only northern Italy now marched forward to an affirmation and realization of cultural achievements; while in France, the Low Countries, Germany, and more or less in all the rest of Europe, culture, though growing, was at the same time floundering and sliding as a result of the progressive weakening of the traditional Mediaeval patterns. This was the period of the north Italian city-states; of growth of commerce and industry, as well as of applied science—spectacles, chimneys, "Arabic" arithmetic and calculation. It was also the time of great Italian literature, painting, architecture, sculpture, then of the foundation of great Italian music—in short, the Renaissance. The beginnings are around 1300, with Dante and Giotto as the symbols—both still Mediaeval in their thinking and feeling, but also initiators of a long line of illustrious personalities whose surge did not begin to enter full culmination until 1500 and was two centuries more in subsiding. This stretch of Italian greatness was achieved wholly without national political unity or military triumphs. It was briefer and more localized than the Mediaeval phase, and thus is perhaps more usefully construed as an interphase transition than as a phase in its own right.

Around 1550 or 1600—perhaps 1575 will serve fairly as a precise definition, though nothing of this sort occurs without gradation—the second main movement in the European symphony began to be played when the other west European countries drew abreast of Italy in wealth, refinement of manners, the arts, and the sciences, after having politically consolidated themselves into organized nation-states. This consolidation gave them a massive weight which before long put them culturally ahead, as regards productivity, of the free but fragmented

Italian cities, or of the "duchies" into which most of these had been transformed or absorbed. Portugal, Spain, Holland, England, France successively achieved this new phase of activity. Meanwhile, with the Reformation, a degree of ideological and emotional autonomy from Italian supremacy was also attained by the northerly nations. This autonomy aided the northern nations, such as Germany, that remained nationalistically or culturally backward, to lay a foundation for greater accomplishment in a subsequent century.

Still later, after about 1750, industrialism, enormously rapid accumulation of wealth, experimental science, democracy and liberalism developed especially in the northwesterly countries, and gave this corner of the continent an increasing precedence of strength, prestige, and influence, in which America came to share and, quite recently, to predominate. Now, this shift is fully familiar; also, like everything that touches us immediately, it is difficult to appraise in historical perspective. A complete understanding of this shift, if it could be attained, would no doubt be full of implications as to the future of our Western civilization—as to its "fate." But that is just what we are not considering at the moment when we are trying to define the *known* boundaries and organization of our civilization, not to guess or argue its future.

The upshot of our review, then, is this. Western Civilization has throughout been multinational and Christian. After a gestatory period of some centuries, it entered a first full phase of about four hundred years in which all higher achievements were meshed into religion. This was the time of culmination of not only the church as an ecclesiastical institution but of Christianity as an ideology and affective nexus. There followed a two or two-and-a-half century period of transition in which many or most of the patterns of this first phase were increasingly loosened and softened, while a set of modified or new patterns gradually formed which were to characterize the subsequent second or Modern phase. Creative cultural leadership in both phases was Transalpine, mostly centering in or near France; in the intervening transition time the leadership and influence were strikingly Cisalpine.[7]

Italy as a segment of Western civilization thus culminated while the remainder of the West was formally uncreative through being in meta-

7. Except for a definite trickle down the Rhine into the Low Countries.

morphosis. But, as the northern and western countries got their second-phase patterns organized, by about 1575, Italy receded in innovation and influence. Italy's peculiar role within the civilization seems bound up first with its having been the political and prestige center of the last phase of the preceding Graeco-Roman civilization, with consequent tendency to retain remnants or remembrances of that civilization. Second, Italian particularity seems connected with having, perhaps on account of its retentions, resisted with a measure of success full acceptance of the High Mediaeval patterns with their barbarian Transalpine provenience and "Gothic" feudal and non-Classical quality. And third, as these patterns were nevertheless at last partly accepted in Italy, but, by a sophisticated population which had never wholly left its towns, they blended with the vestiges and occasional recoveries[8] of the former civilization on the same soil, and above all with the now unleashed creative energies of the people, and put Italy transiently into the van of Western civilization. At about the time when the impulses of this spurt were waning, the Transalpine peoples had begun to formulate their new patterns—such as a dissenting cast of anticlerical Christianity, geographical discovery and expansion, centralized monarchy of power, noticeable accumulation of wealth. Blending with these what they took over from High Renaissance Italy in patterns of manners and art—as Italy had previously accepted some of their Mediaevalism—these northern and western nations attained to the full second phase of Western civilization. This phase in turn, from about 1750–1800 on, spread toward the margins of Europe—Germany, Scandinavia, the Slavic areas—and into the Americas.

If this characterization of the salient physiognomy of Western culture history is essentially correct, it has certain implications of a general and theoretical nature. Such general implications may be more important than even successful close-up predictions would be. The implications may in fact be what in the end will contribute most to our capacity to predict reliably. What this formulation shows is that the

8. This incidental or secondary element of rediscovery or revivification is what has given the Italian cultural surge the name of Renaissance. It was of course far more a birth than a rebirth; but there is some minor ingredient of the latter, as there is of persistence from Graeco-Roman civilization.

course of a large multinational civilization may be more complex than a smooth rise-culmination-and-decline; that it may come in successive surges or pulses—what we have called phases. It is further plain, so far as the preceding formulation is sound, that the intervals between the pulses may be, at least over most of the area of the civilization, periods of pattern dissolution, preparatory to pattern reconstruction. Consequently, even if the mid-twentieth century is suffering from a breakdown of its cultural patterns—as is so often alleged and perhaps with most force and reason as regards the arts—the question still remains open whether such a breakdown is part of the final death of our civilization, as is sometimes feared or asserted; or on the contrary is merely symptomatic of an interpulse reconstruction. In the former case, Spengler's prophecies and Toynbee's fears would be right; in the latter, the present time would be only a sort of counterpart of what Transalpine Europe—most of Europe—was undergoing during the Italian Renaissance.

This question cannot be answered off-handedly in the context of the moment; and even less properly ought a too sure answer be given it at any time. The points to be summarized at this stage of our argument are essentially these. First, it is clear that civilizations are not simple, natural units that are easy to distinguish, or that segregate themselves out from the continuum of history on mere inspection. Second, the duration limits of any one civilization, the points of its beginning and ending, may also be far from easy to define. Instead of being something one begins with as evident, determination of the limits may be a problem in itself. If Toynbee can recognize China I and II and India I and II, why can we not recognize Western I and II?—with perhaps a Western III about to follow? Especially so since it is customary to accept without qualms Egypt *a*, *b*, *c*, *d*, even though not quite separate Egypts I, II, III, and IV. For all that has yet been shown one way or the other, the future may have in store not only Western III but perhaps even IV. In that event, our troubles of today would prove, when the full record shall be in, to be the reconstructive or the growing pains of the transition between phase II that ended say with the nineteenth century and a phase III that will perhaps reach its full beginning in the twenty-first.

Offhand, indeed, Western I and Western II—Mediaeval and Modern Europe—would seem probably to differ more in their patterns than China I from China II. That is, T'ang-Ming China would appear a less altered continuation of Shang-Han China, in spite of its addition of the new religion of Buddhism, than Modern Europe is a continuation of Mediaeval Europe even though Christianity was maintained through both. To be sure, what is foreign and remote always seems more uniform and more continuous than the familiar. Accordingly a careful judicial weighing after intimate acquaintance with both sets of civilizations—if anyone possesses an equally sensitive acquaintance—might conceivably reverse the impression and leave us with the finding that Europe did indeed constitute a single though double-phase civilization, but that China was better construed as two successive civilizations, as Toynbee has it. Yet who could today press with honest assurance for the greater historic truth of either of the two alternatives? The problem is one of estimating the relative degree of difference between complex value-systems. For those interested in such judgments, it is intellectually fair and profitable to form impressions and opinions, but not to assert them beyond tentativeness. All we can really do at present is to ask ourselves questions of this kind, perhaps adding hesitant suggestions of answers. When a number of equipped minds shall have weighed the relevant evidence for perhaps some decades, their findings will carry real weight.

But, as long as we are essentially only asking, we can even now push our questioning farther. If we grant Toynbee's China I and II, and India I and II, and Mesopotamia I and II;[9] and if we are ready to concede at any rate the possibility that the unity of Western civilization may properly be dissolved into Europe I and II; then why should not the taken-for-granted unit which Toynbee calls "Hellenic" civilization and Spengler "Classical"—why should not this be broken into its Greek and Roman components—in parallel terminology, Graeco-Roman I and II?

9. Spengler simplifies the situation by recognizing only the "I" of China, India, and Mesopotamia, approximately, and refusing to discuss the "II's" as being merely frozen "civilizations," fellaheen petrifactions without living culture. But of course this is equivalent to recognizing the "II's." It is not their existence that Spengler denies—only their reaching a certain threshold of cultural worth.

For that matter, genuine consideration could be given this taxonomy:

Aegean = Northeast Mediterranean civilization I
Greek = Northeast Mediterranean civilization II
Roman = Northeast Mediterranean civilization III
Byzantine = Northeast Mediterranean civilization IV

The four would be phases of one localized continuum of civilization that lasted no longer than the continuity of China or India or Mesopotamia or Egypt.[10]

It is evident, I hope, that we are in the stage of seeing problems such as these, indeed of having them forced on the attention; even though our verdicts remain as undogmatic as possible.

In the face of these larger problems, let us then leave the question of when Western civilization will end, or whether it has already begun to end, and of how many stages, phases, or movements it will have consisted when it has terminated—let us leave these problematical matters to the future to which they belong. We can summarize our findings on the completed segments of Western civilization somewhat like this:

500/700–900±. Prodromal stage. Pre-national; Christianity still developing its root system; cultural patterns unformed.

900±-1325±. First phase, Mediaeval. Nationalities present but little organized politically; culmination of Christianity; other culture, so far as well-patterned, saturated with Christianity.

1325±–1575±. Transition, Renaissance in Italy; loosening and reconstitution of culture patterns in Transalpine Europe.

1575±– ? . Second phase, Modern. Nationalities politically organized; culture patterns founded on those of First phase but reformulated secularly, and of wider range.

? (1900?)– ? . Commencing disintegration of whole civilization? Or second transition to a third phase?

10. This interpretation has been developed in Configurations, pages 687–695, 1944.

Made in the USA
Las Vegas, NV
30 October 2024

10663995R00057